A MEMOIR OF
OF THE WAR FO
IN
CONFEDERATE STATES OF AMERICA

MW00478370

American Civil War Classics
Gary W. Gallagher and Robert K. Krick

A Memoir of the Last Year of the War for Independence, in the Confederate States of America, Containing an Account of the Operations of His Commands in the Years 1864 and 1865

JUBAL A. EARLY

WITH A NEW INTRODUCTION BY
Gary W. Gallagher

University of South Carolina Press

UNIVERSITY OF SOUTH CAROLINA *BICENTENNIAL*

© 2001 University of South Carolina

Published in Columbia, South Carolina, by the
University of South Carolina Press

Manufactured in the United States of America

05   04   03   02   01   5   4   3   2   1

Library of Congress Cataloging-in-Publication Data

Early, Jubal Anderson, 1816–1894.
  A memoir of the last year of the War for Independence, in the
Confederate States of America : containing an account of the
operations of his commands in the years 1864 and 1865 / Jubal A.
Early ; with a new intorduction by Gary W. Gallagher.
    p. cm. — (American Civil War classics)
  Originally published: Toronto : Lovell & Gibson, 1866.
  ISBN 1-57003-450-8 (alk. paper)
  1. Early, Jubal Anderson, 1816–1894. 2. United States—History—
Civil War, 1861–1865—Campaigns. 3. United States—History—Civil
War 1861–1865—Personal narratives, Confederate. 4. Generals—
Confederate States of America—Biography. 5. Confederate States of
America. Army—Biography. I. Title. II. Series.
E470.2.E13 2001
973.7'37–dc21   2001052287

CONTENTS

SERIES EDITOR'S PREFACE

Personal narratives by important actors in Civil War scenes afford a fascinating perspective. In the fourteen decades that have elapsed since 1861, memoirs by scores of the war's leading figures have reached print. General Jubal A. Early's *A Memoir of the Last Year of the War for Independence in the Confederate States of America*, released in 1866, was the first such published account by a prominent officer of either side. Accordingly, Early's book not only deserves designation as an American Civil War Classic, but as the *first* classic in a major genre.

Memoirs also, however, inevitably carry the baggage of individual perspective—occasional flashes of limited vision, special pleading, and personal emphases. Even the most determinedly honest and forthright witness, when narrating events in which he played an essential role, writes under a lamp whose glow lights only a portion of his subject.

These characteristics of memoirs make timeliness of authorship of special consequence. The passage of time following momentous military events always generates variant viewpoints, and these often harden into controversial positions, by turns ardently held and vigorously assailed. Contemporary narratives, penned in advance of postwar elaborations, provide especially fresh and valuable material. *A Memoir of the Last Year of the War* meets that criterion most emphatically. Because Early became a leading (perhaps the leading) Confederate controversialist in later decades, his memoir, published just a few months after the events it covers, provides an invaluable perspective. Interestingly, General Early clung tenaciously for thirty years to most of the positions he staked out in 1866.

In addition to its notable "first" cachet, *A Memoir of the Last Year of the War* carries a unique imprimatur: General R. E. Lee corresponded with Early about the book, and read it in draft. Lee died soon after the war, well before the period of intense controversies

that followed (in which he would have been loath to engage had
he lived). Early's book is the only major text that reflects Lee's
personal involvement. Professor Gallagher, who is currently put-
ting the finishing touches on the first serious scholarly biography
of Early, due to be published in 2003, is uniquely equipped to
introduce the general's work.

The American Civil War Classics series will make available
again the voices of the war's participants and eyewitnesses. It is
especially appropriate that the inaugural volume in the series
reprints the first personal narrative published by a major figure.

ROBERT K. KRICK

INTRODUCTION

Former Confederates faced a bleak physical and emotional landscape in the aftermath of Appomattox. Soundly defeated by United States military forces during a four-year struggle that had extracted an enormous human and material toll, they grudgingly acknowledged their failure to establish a slaveholding republic and looked to an uncertain future. Emancipation, an outcome of the war that fueled widespread bitterness against the North, severely threatened the South's social structure, and few white Southerners believed their antebellum ruling class would soon regain political power. Perhaps most tellingly, many civilians and soldiers wondered if their struggle, which had resulted in the loss of hundreds of thousands of dead and maimed men as well as untold material destruction and profound psychological dislocation, had been utterly in vain. "We are *crushed!* subjugated! and I fear, O how I fear, *conquered*," wrote a North Carolina woman who gave voice to widely held sentiments in May 1865. Sensing resignation in the face of unalloyed failure, she worried that the "the lives laid down" would be "as water spilled on the ground," and offered a passionate lament: "O my Country, my Country, I look forward to the future with bitter forebodings when I see your children thus forgetful of your and their own *honour*, of their own *blood!*"[1]

No one surpassed Jubal Anderson Early in his determination to see that the Confederate war would be remembered throughout history as a gallant effort. Early had played a leading role in the Southern military effort. A native of Virginia and graduate of West Point in the class of 1837, he had fought in the Mexican-American War but spent most of his antebellum career practicing law. He described himself as a conservative Whig who, as a delegate to the Virginia state convention in the spring of 1861, strongly opposed secession. After Abraham Lincoln's call for 75,000 volunteers to suppress the rebellion following the firing on Fort Sumter in April 1861 prompted Virginia to leave the Union, Early, though an opponent of secession to the end, quickly offered his services to the fledgling Confederate government. Over the next three years, he participated in all of the great campaigns in the Eastern Theater, playing key roles at First Manassas, Cedar Mountain, Antietam, Chancellorsville, Gettysburg, and the battles of the Overland campaign in May 1864. Robert E. Lee formed a high opinion of Early—whom the Southern soldiers called "Old Jube" or "Old Jubilee"—giving him difficult assignments that required a high degree of autonomy. "[Early's] native intellect, his mental training, his sagacity, his resource, his self-reliant, self-directing strength, were all very great," wrote one Confederate artillerist, "and the commanding general reposed the utmost confidence in him. This he indicated by selecting him so frequently for independent command, and to fill the most critical, difficult, and I had almost said hopeless, positions, in the execution of his own great plans."[2]

Lee also liked Early, though the two men offered a striking contrast in temperament and manners. Lee embodied the white South's ideal of the pious, modest gentleman, whereas Early earned a deserved reputation as one of the most profane officers in the Confederate high command, an individual of well-known skepticism about overly devout compatriots and one whose bitingly sarcastic wit, expressed both on paper and in conversation, found many targets and made many enemies. Early harbored few illusions about himself, confessing after the war that he was "never what is called a popular man." Yet Lee demonstrated obvious affection for his lieutenant, as well as a flash of his sense of humor, in referring to the younger Early as "My bad old man."[3]

Lee's strongest expression of confidence in Early's martial gifts came in June 1864 when he instructed him to mount an independent operation in the Shenandoah Valley. Over the ensuing four months, Early's little Army of the Valley marched more than 1,600 miles, won a number small engagements, and carried the war across the Potomac River and to the outskirts of Washington before suffering shattering defeats at the hands of Philip H. Sheridan's far more powerful Army of the Shenandoah in the battles of Third Winchester, Fisher's Hill, and Cedar Creek between 19 September and 19 October. Early's accomplishments in the 1864 Valley Campaign compared favorably in many respects to "Stonewall" Jackson's fabled operations on the same strategic stage in 1862, but ultimate defeat left him one of the most maligned military figures in the Confederacy. He lingered in the Valley until early March 1865, when he suffered a final ignominious rout at the battle of Waynesboro. An officer from South Carolina reacted to news of what he termed "Early's last disaster in the valley" with words that echoed opinions expressed in newspapers and private correspondence across the Confederacy: "[I] believe Early himself was captured. What a pity they did not get him six (6) months ago. It would have been a lucky thing for the country."[4]

Lee reluctantly removed Early from active duty as the war in Virginia entered its last phase. In a letter dated 30 March 1865, Lee explained that the "reverses in the Valley . . . have I fear, impaired your influence both with the people and the soldiers." "While my own confidence in your ability, zeal, and devotion to the cause, is unimpaired," added Lee in gentle language that Early treasured for the rest of his life, "I have nevertheless felt that I could not oppose what seems to be the current of opinion, without injustice to your reputation, and injury to the service."[5] A general without portfolio in April 1865, Early did not witness the ordeal of the Confederate retreat to Appomattox and the surrender of the Army of Northern Virginia.

Defeat left Early deeply angry. Connected through his mother to some of the largest slaveholders in the South, he always had been a staunch believer in slavery. He considered emancipation an abomination, denounced the North for laying waste to much of the Confederacy during the war, and insisted that he could not remain in Virginia. "I cannot live under the same Government with the Yankee," he informed former Confederate general P. G. T. Beauregard in the autumn of 1865, "and in accordance with a long formed determination, I go into voluntary exile rather than submit to the rule of our enemies." Early added that he could not express to Beauregard "the bitter sorrow I feel in seeing our Country prostrate at the feet of our detested foes, . . . and you may rest assured that if an opportunity ever does arise for giving that glorious old battle flag to the breeze again, I shall hasten to range myself under its folds." What Early did not mention to Beauregard was his concern that he might be placed on trial for his role in the burning of Chambersburg, Pennsylvania, by some of his cavalry during the 1864 Valley campaign. Whatever his full motivation for leaving the United States, Early began his exile in the summer of 1865, traveling first to Texas and then to Nassau, Havana, Mexico, and, eventually, Toronto, Canada, where he would remain until returning to Virginia in the spring of 1869.[6]

While in Mexico, Early turned his attention to writing about his campaigns during the last year of the war. Criticisms of his defeat in the Shenandoah Valley continued to sting, and he hoped to make the case that he had performed ably against enormous odds. A pair of letters from Robert E. Lee prompted Early to think of his project as more than an attempt to burnish his own reputation. In November 1865, Lee informed Early that he planned to write a history of the Army of Northern Virginia. Lacking material on the last year of the conflict because so many official papers had been lost during the retreat from Richmond and Petersburg to Appomattox, he asked Early to send copies of any documents relating to his commands during the period 1864–65. Lee's farewell order to the Army of Northern Virginia at Appomattox had alluded to the Union's "overwhelming resources and numbers," and that topic remained much on his mind. He specifically requested information about Early's strengths at battles from the Overland campaign through the end of operations in the Valley. Lee closed his letter with a sentence that anticipated a major theme in almost all of Early's postwar writings: "My only object is to transmit, if possible, the truth to posterity, and do justice to our brave Soldiers."[7]

Lee sent Early another request on 15 March 1866. He wanted "reports of the operations of your Commands, in the Campaign from the Wilderness to Richmond, at Lynchburg, in the Valley, Maryland, &c." as well as all "statistics as regards numbers, destruction of private property by the Federal troops, &c." Preoccupied with what he perceived as a lack of knowledge about the "odds against which we fought," Lee worried that it would "be difficult to get the world to understand" Grant's advantage in men and matériel. As in his letter of the preceding November, Lee raised the issue of what he called the historical "truth" of the Confederacy's war: "I have not thought proper to notice, or even to correct misrepresentations of my words & acts," he stated. "We shall have to be patient, & suffer for awhile at least. . . . At present the public mind is not prepared to receive the truth."[8]

Early fired a preliminary salvo at his old nemesis Sheridan in a newspaper exchange in the winter of 1866, arguing points Lee had raised concerning strengths and casualties. Sheridan claimed that Early's army had lost nearly 27,000 men killed, wounded, and captured in the Valley; Early insisted that he had never commanded as many as 14,000 men and could not have suffered such heavy losses. Early's arithmetic was better, but this narrow debate represented just a step toward his larger goal of creating a written record that would influence both contemporary readers and future generations. By highlighting Sheridan's advantage in manpower and matériel, Early placed his own performance in a more favorable light and upheld the honor of other badly outnumbered Confederates. On behalf of his "down trodden country," Early appealed to "the civilized nations of the earth" not to learn "the history of this struggle from the mouths and pens of our enemies, but . . . [to] wait until the time shall arrive for placing a true history before them."[9]

By May 1866, Early could report to Thomas L. Rosser, a former cavalry subordinate, that he had completed "a history of my campaigns during 1864 and to the close in 1865." Drawing on a "very retentive memory," personal and official papers he carried with him when he left the country, maps and other materials provided by the famous Confederate cartographer Jedediah Hotchkiss, and a detailed diary kept by an officer named William W. Old who had served on his staff, Early had crafted what he described as "a very thorough account" that he believed would "knock a few feathers out [of] Mr. Sheridan's cap." En route to Canada at the time he wrote to Rosser, Early expected to publish his manuscript after he had settled north of the American border.[10]

He reached Canada in August 1866 and set about revising his manuscript in light of correspondence with former Confederate officers. The book went to press by the second week of December. "I wrote it in Mexico & tried to have it published there but failed," Early reported to Colonel Thomas H. Carter, who had commanded the artillery in the Army of the Valley, "and am glad that I did so, as I have since been able to render it more perfect." Early had ordered 1,000 copies and intended to distribute them at no cost rather than "make a speculation of it. . . . I wish to send copies to the principal officers of my command." Beyond the first printing, Early contemplated "having it republished in the South and sold for the benefit of the Memorial Associations which are engaged in taking care of the dead who fell where my commands fought." Turning from his discussion of the book, Early closed with a vituperative swipe at those who would control at least the short-term destiny of Carter and all others who, unlike Early, remained in the South after the end of the war: "I am getting along here quietly, and watching events on the other side of the line. Do you think if the Gates of Hell were spread wide open that it could belch forth such another set of infernal scoundrels as the Yankees?"[11]

A Memoir of the Last Year of the War for Independence, in the Confederate States of America appeared at the end of 1866 from the Toronto printing firm Lovell and Gibson.[12] Dedicated to the "Memory of the Heroic Dead, who fell fighting for Liberty, Right, and Justice," it represented the first book-length reminiscence by a major military figure on either side of the Civil War. Its opening pages underscored Early's unwillingness to let go of wartime bitterness, inveighing against Northern authors whose writings about the war allegedly distorted history and stridently affirming the righteousness of the Confederate cause. Anyone susceptible to the deeply flawed, though admittedly comforting, notion that national scars healed rapidly after Grant and Lee set a conciliatory public example at Appomattox should read Early's book as an example of widely held opinions in the postwar white South. The New York Times noted Early's unrepentant tone in referring to the sentiments of A Memoir of the Last Year of the War as coming from "one who can Neither Forget nor Learn Anything." Even General Lee betrayed mild disapproval in commenting on a draft of the narrative. Lee read the text "with interest" and found that it "corresponds generally with my recollections." He had no objection to Early's publishing the work but did recommend "that while giving facts which you think necessary for your own vindication, that you omit all epithets or remarks calculated to excite bitterness or animosity between different sections of the Country."[13]

Early's book reflected the enormous influence Robert E. Lee exerted over his former lieutenant.[14] Indeed, Lee's letter of 15 March 1866 can be read as an outline for the book, which covered precisely the period Lee discussed, stressed the North's advantage in numbers, and explored depredations committed by United States forces in the Shenandoah Valley. A wish to satisfy Lee's request for details about the period 1864–65, together with a compelling desire to offer a sympathetic reading of the controversial 1864 Valley Campaign, probably prompted Early to publish only a partial account of his wartime service. He had been at work on a full memoir, which he completed while in Canada. The fact that he never published the larger work suggests that he hurried into print only the chapters that would serve Lee's stated needs and deal with the most troubling aspect of his own Confederate career. Ruth H. Early, Jubal's niece, edited the full memoir for publication eighteen years after "Old Jube's" death in 1894, under the title *Lieutenant General Jubal Anderson Early, C.S.A.: Autobiographical Sketch and Narrative of the War between the States.* The text of *A Memoir of the Last Year of the War* appeared almost verbatim as the last twenty-one chapters of the later work.[15]

Early also had taken to heart Lee's express wish to "transmit . . . the truth to posterity." As he later put it in a letter to Lee, "the most that is left to us is the history of our struggle, and I think that ought to be accurately written." Early acknowledged that defeat had cost Confederates "nearly everything but honor, and that should be religiously guarded."[16]

Much of that sense of honor, in Early's view, derived from the odds against which the Confederates had struggled. Although he tended to inflate Northern and underestimate Confederate strength, Early's main point about numbers was unassailable— Grant had enjoyed a dramatic advantage over Lee in 1864–65 and Sheridan an even larger one over Early's army in the Shenandoah Valley. "Could the world be made to comprehend the immense disparity in numbers existing between the troops engaged in . . . [the Valley]," he wrote shortly before publication of *A Memoir of the Last Year of the War*, "it would be amazed at the fact that my small command was able to continue the struggle so long, and its judgment would be that all the honors remained with that command notwithstanding its reverses."[17]

Early's memoir anticipated later arguments from former Confederates who established what is generally known as the Lost Cause tradition. During the decades following Appomattox, these authors promoted a public memory that celebrated the Confederate people's wartime sacrifice. Their recollections, essays, and speeches played down the importance of slavery as a cause of the war, insisted that secession had been constitutional, largely ignored internal divisions that plagued the Confederacy, cast Confederates as the true heirs of the revolutionary generation, accused United States armies of waging brutal war against Confederate civilians as well as against Southern armies, attributed defeat to the Union's deep pool of manpower and material strength, and celebrated Robert E. Lee and his army as the great martial expression of their nation's struggle for independence. Acting from various motives, Lost Cause writers collectively sought to justify their own actions and allow themselves and other former Confederates to find something positive in a struggle that ended in unequivocal failure. They wanted to bequeath to their children and future generations of white southerners a "correct" narrative of the war. Some also tried to create a documentary record that would shape the work of later historians.[18]

No one did more to further the Lost Cause agenda than Jubal Early. Beginning with *A Memoir of the Last Year of the War* and continuing in lectures, other writings, and personal correspondence with like-minded former comrades, Early sought to establish a historical record favorable to the Confederacy. He pounded a relentless drumbeat of several key points: Robert E. Lee towered over all other commanders as the war's most gifted and admirable general; Confederate armies fought valiantly against overwhelming odds; Ulysses S. Grant possessed only a fraction of Lee's ability as a soldier; Stonewall Jackson stood just behind Lee in the Confederate pantheon; military events in Virginia far overshadowed those of all other theaters of combat; and Confederates occupied the high constitutional and moral ground.

Early eventually became widely recognized across the South as an arbiter of questions relating to Confederate military history.

He played the leading role in efforts to isolate James Longstreet—Lee's ranking lieutenant throughout the war—as a traitor to his section because he had dared to criticize Lee in print. Would-be authors took notice of Early's success in savaging a soldier of Longstreet's manifest wartime accomplishments and reputation. Robert Stiles, an artillerist whose recollections frequently have been quoted by several generations of historians, tellingly commented about Early's impact on ex-Confederates who wrote about the war: "[A]s long as 'the old hero' lived, no man ever took up his pen to write a line about the great conflict without the fear of Jubal Early before his eyes."[19]

After more than one hundred thirty years, *A Memoir of the Last Year of the War* remains a valuable title for anyone interested in the Civil War. Most obviously, it explores important battles and campaigns from the perspective of an officer who exerted considerable influence on the course of events in the Eastern Theater. It also provides a fascinating glimpse at the earliest stage of the effort by Lost Cause writers to affect how the conflict would be remembered by those who lived through it and how it would be interpreted by future generations. Early's scarcely concealed biases also underscore that the war had been waged for the highest stakes and had left untold Confederates profoundly embittered. Although his brief narrative will surely win few converts to the Lost Cause point of view, "Old Jube" would likely be pleased to know that it continues to command attention.

NOTES

1. Catherine Ann Devereux Edmondston, *"Journal of a Secesh Lady": The Diary of Catherine Ann Devereux Edmondston*, ed. Beth Gilbert Crabtree and James W. Patton (Raleigh: North Carolina Division of Archives and History, 1979), 708.

2. Robert Stiles, *Four Years Under Marse Robert* (1903; reprint, Dayton, Ohio: Morningside, 1977), 188–89. Early has been the subject of two full-length biographies, Millard K. Bushong's highly laudatory *Old Jube: A Biography of General Jubal A. Early* (Boyce, Va.: Carr Publishing Company, 1955), and Charles C. Osborne's more detailed and critical *Jubal: The Life and Times of General Jubal A. Early, CSA, Defender of the Lost Cause* (Chapel Hill, N.C.: Algonquin Books of Chapel Hill, 1992).

3. Jubal A. Early, *Lieutenant General Jubal Anderson Early, C.S.A.: Autobi-*

ographical Sketch and Narrative of the War Between the States (Philadelphia: J. B. Lippincott, 1912), xxv. For a wartime example of Lee's nickname for Early, see the letter from "Phax" in the *Mobile Advertiser*, 15 September 1864. The only other lieutenant given a nickname by Lee was James Longstreet, whom the commanding general greeted as "My old war horse" on the battlefield at Antietam.

4. John Cheves Haskell to "Dear ma," 5 March 1865, Rachel Susan Cheves Papers, Perkins Library, Duke University, Durham, N.C.

5. R. E. Lee to J. A. Early, 30 March 1865, George H. and Katherine M. Davis Collection, Howard-Tilton Memorial Library, Tulane University, New Orleans, La. (collection cited hereafter as Davis Collection, TU). The punctuation in the original letter differs slightly from that in the version Early included as Appendix A in *A Memoir of the Last Year of the War for Independence, in the Confederate States of America*. On Early's Valley campaign, see Frank E. Vandiver, *Jubal's Raid: General Early's Famous Attack on Washington in 1864* (New York: McGraw-Hill, 1960); Benjamin Franklin Cooling, *Jubal Early's Raid on Washington: 1864* (Baltimore, Md.: Nautical and Aviation Publishing, 1989); and Jeffry D. Wert, *From Winchester to Cedar Creek: The Shenandoah Campaign of 1864* (Carlisle, Pa.: South Mountain Press, 1987).

6. For a concise description of Early's wanderings between 1865 and 1869, see Osborne, *Jubal*, 403–13.

7. R. E. Lee to Jubal A. Early, 22 November 1865, Davis Collection, TU.

8. R. E. Lee to Jubal A. Early, 15 March 15 1866, Davis Collection, TU.

9. Jubal A. Early to Editor of the *New York News*, 5 February 1866, responding to Philip H. Sheridan's letter to Editors of the *New Orleans Daily Crescent*, 8 January 1866, newspaper clippings in Scrapbook, Jubal A. Early Papers, Library of Congress, Washington, D.C.

10. William D. Hoyt Jr., ed., "New Light on General Jubal A. Early After Appomattox," *Journal of Southern History* 9 (February-November 1943): 115–16.

11. Jubal A. Early to Thomas H. Carter, 13 December 1866, Lee Family Papers, 1732–1892, Virginia Historical Society, Richmond, Va. (repository hereafter cited as VHS). Robert E. L. Krick kindly supplied a typescript of this letter.

12. Subsequent editions, each slightly revised, were published in 1867 in New Orleans, La.; Lynchburg, Va.; and Augusta, Ga. As Early had promised in his letter to Thomas H. Carter, all proceeds went to support efforts by ladies' memorial associations. A publisher's note in the Lynchburg edition assured purchasers that profits would be "sacredly appro-

priated" to the "pious task of collecting the remains of the Southern soldiers who fell on Virginia battle-fields, with the view of enclosing and marking their graves."

13. *New York Times*, 26 August 1867, R. E. Lee to Jubal A. Early, 15 October 1868, Davis Collection, TU.

14. Early had exhibited great admiration for Lee even before the Civil War, agreeing with General-in-Chief Winfield Scott and many other Virginians that Lee compiled a brilliant record during the Mexican-American War. Although Early habitually criticized Confederate civilian and military leaders, he never spoke negatively about Lee. "For Lee he seemed to have a regard and esteem and high opinion," remarked one witness who heard Early talk about Lee in 1862, "felt by him for no one else" (John S. Wise, *The End of An Era* [Boston and New York: Houghton Mifflin, 1899], 228). Lee's considerate handling of Early's removal in March 1865 cemented an already profound sense of admiration on the latter's part.

15. J. B. Lippincott of Philadelphia published the full memoir in 1912. The book has been reprinted by Indiana University Press as part of its Civil War Centennial Series, with an introduction by Frank E. Vandiver, under the title *War Memoirs: Autobiographical Sketch and Narrative of the War between the States* (Bloomington, Ind., 1960); Nautical and Aviation Publishing under the title *Jubal Early's Memoirs: Autobiographical Sketch and Narrative of the War between the States*, with an introduction by Craig E. Symonds (Baltimore, Md., 1989); and Broadfoot Publishing Company under the original title, with an introduction by Gary W. Gallagher (Wilmington, N.C., 1989).

16. Jubal A. Early to R. E. Lee, 20 November 1868, box 25, folder titled "Introductory Chapter (Notes & Pages of a Rough Draft) I," John Warwick Daniel Papers, Alderman Library, University of Virginia, Charlottesville.

17. Jubal A. Early to [?], Mss1/N5156/a, Elizabeth Byrd Nicholas Papers, VHS.

18. On the myth of the Lost Cause, see Gaines M. Foster, *Ghosts of the Confederacy: Defeat, the Lost Cause, and the Emergence of the New South, 1865–1913* (New York: Oxford University Press, 1987); Charles Reagan Wilson, *Baptized in Blood: The Religion of the Lost Cause, 1865–1920* (Athens: University of Georgia Press, 1980); and Gary W. Gallagher and Alan T. Nolan, eds., *The Myth of the Lost Cause and Civil War History* (Bloomington: Indiana University Press, 2000).

19. Stiles, *Four Years Under Marse Robert*, 190–91. On Early's role as a Lost Cause warrior, see Thomas L. Connelly, *The Marble Man: Robert E. Lee*

and His Image in American Society (New York: Knopf, 1977), chapters 2–3; Gallagher and Nolan, eds., *The Lost Cause and Civil War History*, chapter 2; and Gary W. Gallagher, *Lee and His Army in Confederate History* (Chapel Hill: University of North Carolina Press, 2001), chapter 8.

PREFACE TO THE FIRST EDITION

Under a solemn sense of duty to my unhappy country, and to the brave soldiers who fought under me, as well as to myself, the following pages have been written.

When the question of practical secession from the United States arose, as a citizen of the State of Virginia, and a member of the Convention called by the authority of the Legislature of that State, I opposed secession with all the ability I possessed, with the hope that the horrors of civil war might be averted, and that a returning sense of duty and justice on the part of the masses of the Northern States, would induce them to respect the rights of the people of the South. While some Northern politicians and editors, who subsequently took rank among the most unscrupulous and vindictive of our enemies, and now hold me to be a traitor and rebel, were openly and sedulously justifying and encouraging secession, I was labouring honestly and earnestly to preserve the Union.

As a member of the Virginia Convention, I voted against the ordinance of secession on its passage by that body, with the hope that, even then, the collision of arms might be avoided, and some satisfactory adjustment arrived at. The adoption of that ordinance wrung from me bitter tears of grief; but I at once recognized my duty to abide the decision of my native State, and to defend her soil against invasion. Any scruples which I may have entertained as to the right of secession, were soon dispelled by the mad, wicked, and unconstitutional measures of the authorities at Washington, and the frenzied clamour of the people of the North for war upon their former brethren of the South. I then, and ever since have, regarded Abraham Lincoln, his counsellors and supporters, as the real traitors who had overthrown the constitution and government of the United States, and established in lieu thereof an odious despotism; and this opinion I entered on the journal of the Convention when I signed the ordinance of secession. I recognized the right of resistance and revolution as exercised by our fathers in 1776, and, without cavil as to the name by which it was called, I entered the military service of my State, willingly, cheerfully, and zealously.

When the State of Virginia became one of the Confederate States, and her troops were turned over to the Confederate Government, I embraced the cause of the whole Confederacy with equal ardour, and continued in the service, with the determination to devote all the energy and talent I possessed to the common defence. I fought through the entire war, without once regretting the course I had pursued; with an abiding faith in the justice of our cause; and I never saw the moment when I would have been willing to consent to any compromise or settlement short of the absolute independence of my country.

It was my fortune to participate in most of the great military operations in which the army in Virginia was engaged, both before and after General Lee assumed the command. In the last year of this momentous struggle, I commanded, at different times, a division and two corps of General Lee's Army, in the campaign from the Rapidan to James River, and, subsequently, a separate force which marched into Maryland, threatened Washington City, and then went through an eventful campaign in the Valley of Virginia. No detailed reports of the operations of these different commands were made before the close of the war, and the campaign in Maryland and the Valley of Virginia has been the subject of much comment and misapprehension. I have now written a narrative of the operations of all my commands during the closing year of the war, and lay it before the world as a contribution to the history of our great struggle for independence. In giving this narrative, I have made such statements of the positions and strength of the opposing forces in Virginia, and such reference to their general operations, as were necessary to enable the reader to understand it; but I do not pretend to detail the operations of other commanders.

I have not found it necessary to be guilty of the injustice of attempting to pull down the reputation of any of my fellow officers, in order to build up my own. My operations and my campaign stand on their own merits, whatever they may be. Nor, in anything I may have found it necessary to say in regard to the conduct of my troops, do I wish to be understood as, in any way, decrying the soldiers who constituted the rank and file of my commands. I believe that the world has never produced a body of men superior, in courage, patriotism, and endurance, to the private soldiers of the Confederate armies. I have repeatedly seen those soldiers submit, with cheerfulness, to privations and hardships which would appear to be almost incredible; and the wild cheers of our brave men, (which were so different from the studied hurrahs of the Yankees,) when their thin lines sent back opposing hosts of Federal troops, staggering, reeling, and flying, have often thrilled every fibre in my heart. I have seen, with my own eyes, ragged, barefooted, and hungry Confederate soldiers perform deeds, which, if performed in days of yore by mailed warriors in glittering armour, would have inspired the harp of the minstrel and the pen of the poet.

I do not aspire to the character of a historian, but, having been a witness of and participator in great events, I have given a statement of what I saw and did, for the use of the future historian. Without breaking the thread of my narrative, as it proceeds, I have given, in notes, comments on some of the errors and inconsistencies committed by the commander of the Federal army, General Grant, and the Federal Secretary of War, Mr. Stanton, in their reports made since the close of the war; also some instances of cruelty and barbarity committed by the Federal commanders, which were brought to my immediate attention, as well as some other matters of interest.

As was to have been expected, our enemies have flooded the press with sketches and histories, in which all the appliances of a meretricious literature have been made use of, to glorify their own cause and its supporters, and to blacken ours. But some Southern writers also, who preferred the pen to the sword or musket, have not been able to resist the temptation to rush into print; and, accordingly, carping criticisms have been written by the light of after events, and even histories of the war attempted by persons, who imagined that the distinctness of their vision was enhanced by distance from the scene of conflict, and an exemption from the disturbing elements of whistling bullets and bursting shells. Perhaps other writers of the same class may follow, and various speculations be indulged in, as to the causes of our disasters. As for myself, I have not undertaken to speculate as to the causes of our failure, as I have seen abundant reason for it in the tremendous odds brought against us. Having had some means of judging, I will, however, say that, in my opinion, both President Davis and General Lee, in their respective spheres, did all for the success of our cause which it was possible for mortal men to do; and it is a great privilege and comfort for me so to believe, and to have been able to bring with me into exile a profound love and veneration for those great men.

In regard to my own services, all I have to say is, that I have the consciousness of having done my duty to my country, to the very best of my ability, and, whatever may be my fate, I would not exchange that consciousness for untold millions. I have come into exile rather than submit to the yoke of the oppressors of my country; but I have never thought of attributing aught of blame or censure to those true men who, after having nobly done their duty in the dreadful struggle through which we passed, now, that it has gone against us, remain to share the misfortunes of their people, and to aid and comfort them in their trials; on the contrary, I appreciate and honor their motives. I have not sought refuge in another land from insensibility to the wrongs and sufferings of my own country; but I feel deeply and continually for them, and could my life secure the redemption of that country, as it has been often risked, so now it would be as freely given for that object.

There were men born and nurtured in the Southern States, and some of them in my own State, who took sides with our enemies, and aided in desolating and humiliating the land of their own birth, and of the graves of their ancestors. Some of them rose to high positions in the United States Army, and others to high civil positions. I envy them not their dearly bought prosperity. I had rather be the humblest private soldier who fought in the ranks of the Confederate Army, and now, maimed and disabled, hobbles on his crutches from house to house, to receive his daily bread from the hands of the grateful women for whose homes he fought, than the highest of those renegades and traitors. Let them enjoy the advantages of their present positions as best they may! for the deep and bitter execrations of an entire people now attend them, and an immortality of infamy awaits them. As for all the enemies who have overrun or aided in overrunning my country, there is a wide and impassable gulf between us, in which I see the blood of slaughtered friends, comrades, and countrymen, which all the waters in the firmament above and the seas beneath cannot wash away. Those enemies have undertaken to render our cause odious and infamous; and among other atrocities committed by them in the effort to do so, an humble subordinate, poor Wirz, has been selected as a victim to a fiendish spirit, and basely murdered under an executive edict, founded on the sentence of a vindictive and illegal tribunal. Let them consider this system! they are but erecting monuments to their own eternal dishonour, and furnishing finger posts to guide the historian in his researches. They may employ the infamous Holt, with his "Bureau of Military Justice," to sacrifice other victims on the altars of their hatred, and provost marshals, and agents of the "Freedman's Bureau" may riot in all the license of petty tyranny, but our enemies can no more control the verdict of impartial history, than they can escape that doom which awaits them at the final judgment.

During the war, slavery was used as a catch-word to arouse the passions of a fanatical mob, and to some extent the prejudices of the civilized world were excited against us; but the war was not made on our part for slavery. High dignitaries in both church and state in Old England, and puritans in New England, had participated in the profits of a trade, by which the ignorant and barbarous natives of Africa were brought from that country, and sold into slavery in the American Colonies. The generation in the Southern States which defended their country in the late war, found amongst them, in a civilized and christianized condition, 4,000,000 of the descendants of those degraded Africans. The Almighty Creator of the Universe had stamped them, indelibly, with a different colour and an inferior physical and mental organization. He had not done this from mere caprice or whim, but for wise purposes. An amalgamation of the races was in contravention of His designs, or He would not have made them so different. This immense number of people could not have been transported back to the wilds from which their ancestors were taken, or if they could have been, it would have resulted in their relapse into barbarism. Reason, common sense, true humanity to the black, as well as the safety of the white race, required that the inferior race should be kept in a state of subordination. The condition of domestic slavery, as it existed in the South, had not only resulted in a great improvement in the moral and physical condition of the negro race, but had furnished a class of labourers as happy and contented as any in the world, if not more so. Their labour had not only developed the immense resources of the immediate country in which they were located, but was the main source of the great prosperity of the United States, and furnished the means for the employment of millions of the working classes in other countries. Nevertheless, the struggle made by the people of the South was not for the institution of slavery, but for the inestimable right of self-government, against the domination of a fanatical faction at the North; and slavery was the mere occasion of the development of the antagonism between the two sections. That right of self-government has been lost, and slavery violently abolished. Four millions of blacks have thus been thrown on their own resources, to starve, to die, and to relapse into barbarism; and inconceivable miseries have been entailed on the white race.

The civilized world will find, too late, that its philanthropy has been all false, and its religion all wrong on this subject; and the people of the United States will find that, under the pretence of "saving the life of the nation, and upholding the old flag," they have surrendered their own liberties into the hands of that worst of all tyrants, a body of senseless fanatics.

When the passions and infatuations of the day shall have been dissipated by time, and all the results of the late war shall have passed into irrevocable history, the future chronicler of that history will have a most important duty to perform, and posterity, while pouring over its pages, will be lost in wonder at the follies and crimes committed in this generation.

My narrative is now given to the public, and the sole merit I claim for it is that of truthfulness. In writing it, I have received material aid from an accurate diary kept by Lieutenant William W. Old, aide to Major General Edward Johnson, who was with me during the campaign in Maryland and the Shenandoah Valley until the 12th of August, 1864, and the copious notes of Captain J. Hotchkiss, who acted as Topographical Engineer for the 2nd

Corps and the Army of the Valley District, and recorded the events of each day, from the opening of the campaign on the Rapidan in May, 1864, until the affair at Waynesboro in March, 1865.

J. A. EARLY.
November, 1866.

CAMPAIGN IN VIRGINIA,

FROM THE

RAPIDAN TO JAMES RIVER.

INTRODUCTION.

On the 3rd of May, 1864, the positions of the Confederate
Army under General Lee, and the Federal Army under Lieu-
tenant-General Grant, in Virginia, were as follows: General
Lee held the southern bank of the Rapidan River, in Orange
County, with his right resting near the mouth of Mine Run,
and his left extending to Liberty Mills on the road from
Gordonsville (via Madison Court House) to the Shenandoah
Valley ; while the crossings of the river on the right, and the
roads on the left were watched by cavalry: Ewell's corps
was on the right, Hill's on the left, and two divisions of Longstreet's corps were encamped in the rear, near Gordonsville.
Grant's army (composed of the Army of the Potomac under
Meade, and the 9th corps under Burnside,) occupied the north
banks of the Rapidan and Robinson rivers ; the main body
being encamped in Culpepper County, and on the Rappahannock River.

I am satisfied that General Lee's army did not exceed
50,000 effective men of all arms. The report of the Federal
Secretary of War, Stanton, shows that the " available force
present for duty, May 1st 1864," in Grant's army, was 141,166,
to wit : In the Army of the Potomac 120,386, and in the 9th
corps 20,780. The draft in the United States was being
energetically enforced, and volunteering had been greatly

stimulated by high bounties. The North-Western States had tendered large bodies of troops to serve one hundred days, in order to relieve other troops on garrison and local duty, and this enabled Grant to put in the field a large number of troops which had been employed on that kind of duty. It was known that he was receiving heavy reinforcements up to the very time of his movement on the 4th of May, and afterwards ; so that the statement of his force on the 1st of May, by Stanton, does not cover the whole force with which he commenced the campaign. Moreover, Secretary Stanton's report shows that there were, in the Department of Washington and the Middle Department, 47,751 available men for duty, the chief part of which, he says, was called to the front after the campaign began, " in order to repair the losses of the Army of the Potomac ;" and Grant says that, at Spottsylvania Court House, "the 13th, 14th, 15th, 16th, 17th, and 18th [of May,] were consumed in manœuvring and awaiting the arrival of reinforcements from Washington." His army, therefore, must have numbered very nearly, if not quite, 200,000 men, before a junction was effected with Butler.

On the 4th of May, it was discovered that Grant's Army was moving towards Germana Ford on the Rapidan, which was ten or twelve miles from our right. This movement had begun on the night of the 3rd, and the enemy succeeded in seizing the ford, and effecting a crossing, as the river was guarded at that point by only a small cavalry picket. The direct road from Germana Ford to Richmond passes by Spottsylvania Court House, and when Grant had effected his crossing, he was nearer to Richmond than General Lee was. From Orange Court House, near which were General Lee's headquarters, there are two nearly parallel roads running eastwardly to Fredericksburg—the one which is nearest to the river being called " The old Stone Pike," and the other " The Plank Road." The road from Germana Ford to Spottsylvania Court House, crosses the old Stone Pike at the " Old Wilderness Tavern," and two or three miles further on, it crosses the Plank Road.

As soon as it was ascertained that Grant's movement was a serious one, preparations were made to meet him, and the troops of General Lee's Army were put in motion—Ewell's corps moving on the old Stone Pike, and Hill's corps on the Plank Road; into which latter road Longstreet's force also came, from his camp near Gordonsville.

Ewell's corps, to which my division belonged, crossed Mine Run, and encamped at Locust Grove, four miles beyond, on the afternoon of the 4th. When the rest of the corps moved, my division and Ramseur's brigade of Rodes' division were left to watch the fords of the Rapidan, until relieved by cavalry. As soon as this was done, I moved to the position occupied by the rest of the corps, carrying Ramseur with me.

Ewell's corps contained three divisions of infantry, to wit: Johnson's, Rodes', and my own (Early's). At this time, one of my brigades (Hoke's) was absent, having been with Hoke in North Carolina; and I had only three present, to wit: Hays', Pegram's, and Gordon's. One of Rodes' brigades (R. D. Johnston's) was at Hanover Junction. I had about 4,000 muskets for duty; Johnson about the same number; and Rodes (including Johnston's brigade) about 6,000.

BATTLES OF THE WILDERNESS.

On the morning of the 5th, Ewell's corps was put in motion, my division bringing up the rear. A short distance from the Old Wilderness Tavern, and just in advance of the place where a road diverges to the left from the old Stone Pike to the Germana Ford road, the enemy, in heavy force, was encountered, and Jones' brigade, of Johnson's division, and Battle's brigade, of Rodes' division, were driven back in some confusion. My division was ordered up, and formed across the pike; Gordon's brigade being on the right of the road. This brigade, as soon as it was brought into line, was ordered forward, and advanced, through a dense pine thicket, in gallant style. In conjunction with Daniels', Doles', and Ramseur's brigades, of Rodes' division, it drove the enemy back with heavy loss, capturing several hundred prisoners, and gaining a commanding position on the right. Johnson, at the same time, was heavily engaged in his front; his division being on the left of the pike, and extending across the road to the Germana Ford road, which has been mentioned. After the enemy had been repulsed, Hays' brigade was sent to Johnson's left, in order to participate in a forward movement; and it did move forward, some half-a-mile or so, encountering the enemy in force; but, from some mistake, not meeting with the expected co-operation, except from one regiment of Jones' brigade (the 25th. Va.), the most of which was captured, it was drawn back to Johnson's line, and took position on his left.

Pegram's brigade was subsequently sent to take position on Hays' left; and, just before night, a very heavy attack was made on its front, which was repulsed with severe loss to the enemy. In this affair, General Pegram received a severe wound in the leg, which disabled him for the field for some months.

During the afternoon there was heavy skirmishing along the whole line, several attempts having been made by the enemy, without success, to regain the position from which he had been driven ; and the fighting extended to General Lee's right, on the Plank Road. Gordon occupied the position which he had gained, on the right, until after dark, when he was withdrawn to the extreme left, and his place occupied by part of Rodes' division.

The troops encountered, in the beginning of the fight, consisted of the 5th. corps, under Warren ; but other troops were brought to his assistance. At the close of the day, Ewell's corps had captured over a thousand prisoners, besides inflicting on the enemy very heavy losses in killed and wounded. Two pieces of artillery had been abandoned by the enemy, just in front of the point at which Johnson's right and Rodes' left joined, and were subsequently secured by our troops.

After the withdrawal of Gordon's brigade from the right, the whole of my division was on the left of the road diverging from the pike, in extension of Johnson's line. All my brigades had behaved handsomely ; and Gordon's advance, at the time of the confusion, in the beginning of the fight, was made with great energy and dispatch, and was just in time to prevent a serious disaster.

Early on the morning of the 6th, the fighting was resumed, and a very heavy attack was made on the front occupied by Pegram's brigade (now under the command of Colonel Hoffman, of the 31st Virginia Regiment) ; but it was handsomely repulsed, as were several subsequent attacks at the same point.

These attacks were so persistent, that two regiments of Johnson's division were moved to the rear of Pegram's brigade, for the purpose of supporting it ; and, when an offer was made to relieve it, under the apprehension that its ammunition might be exhausted, the men of that gallant brigade begged that they might be allowed to retain their position, stating that they were getting along very well indeed, and wanted no help.

During the morning, the fact was communicated to General Ewell, by our cavalry scouts, that a column of the enemy's infantry was moving between our left and the river, with the apparent purpose of turning our left flank ; and information was also received that Burnside's corps had crossed the river, and was in rear of the enemy's right. I received directions to watch this column, and take steps to prevent its getting to our rear ; and Johnston's brigade, of Rodes' division, which had just arrived from Hanover Junction, was sent to me for that purpose. This brigade, with some artillery, was put in position, some distance to my left, so as to command some bye-roads coming in from the river. In the meantime General Gordon had sent out a scouting party on foot, which discovered what was supposed to be the enemy's right flank resting in the woods, in front of my division ; and, during my absence while posting Johnston's brigade, he reported the fact to General Ewell, and suggested the propriety of attacking this flank of the enemy with his brigade, which was not engaged. On my return, the subject was mentioned to me by General Ewell, and I stated to him the danger and risk of making the attack under the circumstances, as a column was threatening our left flank, and Burnside's corps was in rear of the enemy's flank on which the attack was suggested. General Ewell concurred with me in this opinion, and the impolicy of the attempt at that time was obvious, as we had no reserves, and, if it failed, and the enemy showed any enterprise, a serious disaster would befall, not only our corps, but General Lee's whole army. In the afternoon, when the column threatening our left had been withdrawn, and it had been ascertained that Burnside had gone to Grant's left, on account of the heavy fighting on that flank, at my suggestion, General Ewell ordered the movement which Gordon had proposed. I determined to make it with Gordon's brigade supported by Johnston's, and to follow it up, if successful, with the rest of my division. Gordon's brigade was accordingly formed in line near the edge of the woods in which the enemy's right rested, and Johnston's in the rear, with orders to follow Gordon and obey his orders. I posted my Adjutant General, Major John W. Daniel, with a courier, in a position to be communicated with by Gordon, so as to inform me of the success attending the movement, and enable me to put in the other brigades at the right time. As soon as Gordon started, which was a very short time before sunset, I rode to my line and threw forward Pegram's brigade in a position to move when required. In the meantime Gordon had become engaged, and, while Pegram's brigade was being formed in line, I saw some of Gordon's men coming back in confusion, and Colonel Evans, of the 31st Georgia Regiment, endeavoring to rally them. Colonel Evans informed me that his regiment, which was on Gordon's right, had struck the enemy's breastworks and had given way. I immediately ordered Pegram's brigade forward, and directed Colonel Evans to guide it. Its advance was through a dense thicket of underbrush, but it crossed the road running through Johnson's line, and struck the enemy's works, and one of the regiments, the 13th Virginia, under Colonel Terrill, got possession of part of the line, when Colonel Hoffman ordered the brigade to retire, as it was getting dark, and there was much confusion produced by the difficulties of the advance. Gordon had struck the enemy's right flank behind breastworks, and a part of his brigade was thrown into disorder. In going through the woods, Johnston had obliqued too much and passed to Gordon's left, getting in rear of the enemy. Major Daniel, not hearing from Gordon, had endeavored to get to him, when, finding the condition of things, he attempted to lead one of Pegram's regiments to his assistance, and was shot down while behaving with great gallantry, receiving a wound in the leg which has permanently disabled him. Notwithstanding the confusion in part of his brigade, Gordon succeeded in throwing the enemy's right flank into great confusion, capturing two brigadier generals (Seymour and Shaler), and several hundred prisoners, all of the 6th Corps, under

Sedgwick. The advance of Pegram's brigade, and the demonstration of Johnston's brigade in the rear, where it encountered a part af the enemy's force and captured some prisoners, contributed materially to the result. It was fortunate, however, that darkness came to close this affair, as the enemy, if he had been able to discover the disorder on our side, might have brought up fresh troops and availed himself of our condition. As it was, doubtless, the lateness of the hour caused him to be surprised, and the approaching darkness increased the confusion in his ranks, as he could not see the strength of the attacking force, and probably imagined it to be much more formidable than it really was. All of the brigades engaged in the attack were drawn back, and formed on a new line in front of the old one, and obliquely to it.

At light on the morning of the 7th, an advance was made, which disclosed the fact that the enemy had given up his line of works in front of my whole line, and a good portion of Johnson's. Between the lines, a large number of his dead had been left, and, at his breastworks, a large number of muskets and knapsacks had been abandoned, and there was every indication of great confusion. It was not till then, that we ascertained the full extent of the success attending the movement of the evening before. The enemy had entirely abandoned the left side of the road, across which Johnson's line extended, and my division and a part of his were thrown forward, occupying a part of the abandoned works on the right of the road, and leaving all those on the left in our rear. This rendered our line straight, the left having been previously thrown back, making a curve.

During this day there was some skirmishing, but no serious fighting in my front. The loss in my division during the fighting in the Wilderness was comparatively light.

On the morning of the 8th, it was discovered that the enemy was leaving our front and moving towards Spottsylvania Court House. General Lee's army was also put in motion ; Ewell's Corps moving along the line occupied by our troops on the day before, until it reached the Plank Road, where it struck across to Shady Grove, which is on the road from Orange Court House to Spottsylvania Court House.

On reaching the Plank Road, I received through General A. P. Hill, who was sick and unable to remain on duty, an order from General Lee, transferring Hays' brigade from my division to Johnson's, in order that it might be consolidated with another Louisiana brigade in that division, whose Brigadier-General had been killed at the Wilderness, and Johnston's brigade from Rodes' division to mine ; and assigning me to the temporary command of Hill's corps, which was still in position across the Plank Road, and was to bring up the rear. I accordingly turned over the command of my division to Gordon, the senior Brigadier left with it, and assumed command of Hill's corps.*

---

*In his official report. Grant says : " Early on the 5th, the advance corps, the 5th, Major-General G. K. Warren commandiug, met and engaged the enemy outside his entrenchments near Mine Run ; " and further on he says : " On the morning of the 7th, reconnoissances showed that the enemy had fallen behind his entrenched lines, with pickets to the front covering a part of the battle field. From this it was evident to my mind that the two days fighting had satisfied him of his inability to further maintain the contest in the open field, notwithstanding his advantage of position, and that he would wait an attack behind his works " In mentioning his movement towards Spottsylvania Court House, he says : " But the enemy having become aware of our movement, and having the shorter line, was enabled to reach there first." If these statements were true, the only legitimate inference is that General Lee had an entrenched line on, or near Mine Run, previously established ; that the battle commenced immediately in front of the works on this line ; and that, after the two days fighting, he had fallen behind them to await an attack. Whereas the fact is, that the only entrenched line on, or near, Mine Run, was that made, on its west bank, when Meade crossed the river at the end of November 1863, and which was used for that occasion only. The fighting in the Wilderness began eight or ten miles east of that line, and at no time during that fighting was it used for any purpose. The ' entrenched lines " occupied by our army on the morning of the 7th, were slight temporary works thrown up, on, or in front of the battle field, though it is probable that, at some points, the line may not have been as far to the front as our troops had advanced ; as, in taking it, regard was necessarily had to the conformation of the ground. On our left, as will be seen above, the line was advanced in front of Grant's own line of the previous day.

Grant says General Lee had the advantage of position As the latter had to move from his lines on the Rapidan and attack Grant in the Wilderness, how

BATTLES AROUND SPOTTSYLVANIA COURT HOUSE.

OPERATIONS OF HILL'S CORPS.

Hill's Corps was composed of Heth's, Wilcox's, and Mahone's (formerly Anderson's) divisions of infantry, and three battalions of artillery under Colonel Walker. When I took command of it, the infantry numbered about 13,000 muskets for duty.

General Lee's orders to me, were to move by Todd's tavern along the Brock Road to Spottsylvania Court House, as soon as our front was clear of the enemy. In order to get into that road, it was necessary to reopen an old one leading from Hill's right, by which I was enabled to take a cross road leading into the road from Shady Grove to Todd's tavern. The waggon trains and all the artillery, except one battalion, were sent around by Shady Grove. About a mile from the road from Shady Grove to Todd's tavern, the enemy's cavalry videttes were encountered, and Mahone's division was thrown forward to develope the enemy's force and position. Mahone encountered a force of infantry, which had moved up from Todd's tavern towards Shady Grove, and had quite a brisk engagement with it, causing it to fall back rapidly towards the former place. At the same time, General Hampton, who had communicated with me, after I left the Plank Road, moved with his cavalry on my right and struck

happened it that he was enabled to get the advantage of position, after the two days fighting? He also says that General Lee was enabled to reach Spottsylvania Court House, first, because he had the shorter line. The fact is, that, as the two armies lay in their positions at the Wilderness, their lines were parallel to the road to Spottsylvania Court House. Grant had the possession of the direct road to that place, and he had the start. General Lee had to move on the circuitous route by Shady Grove, and he was enabled to arrive there first with part of his infantry, because his cavalry held Grant's advance in check for nearly an entire day.

the enemy on the flank and rear; but on account of want of knowledge of the country on our part, and the approach of darkness, the enemy was enabled to make his escape. This affair developed the fact that the enemy was in possession of Todd's tavern and the Brock Road, and a continuation of my march would have led though his entire army. We bivouacked for the night, at the place from which Mahone had driven the enemy, and a force was thrown out towards Todd's tavern, which was about a mile distant.

Very early next morning, (the 9th,) I received an order from General Lee, through Hampton, to move on the Shady Grove road towards Spottsylvannia Court House, which I did, crossing a small river called the Po, twice. After reaching the rear of the position occupied by the other two corps, I was ordered to Spottsylvannia Court House, to take position on the right, and cover the road from that place to Fredericksburg. No enemy appeared in my front on this day, except at a distance on the Fredericksburg Road.

Early on the morning of the 10th, I was ordered to move one of my divisions back, to cover the crossing of the Po on the Shady Grove Road; and to move with another division, to the rear and left, by the way of Spottsylvannia Old Court House, and drive back a column of the enemy which had crossed the Po and taken possession of the Shady Grove Road, thus threatening our rear and endangering our trains, which were on the road leading by the Old Court House to Louisa Court House.

Our line was then north of the Po, with its left, Fields' division of Longstreet's corps, resting on that stream, just above the crossing of the Shady Grove Road. The whole of the enemy's force was also north of the Po, prior to this movement of his. Mahone's division was sent to occupy the banks of the Po on Field's left, while, with Heth's division and a battalion of artillery, I moved to the rear, crossing the Po on the Louisa Court House Road, and then following that road until we reached one coming in from Waite's Shop on the Shady Grove Road. After moving about a mile on this

road, we met Hampton gradually falling back before the
enemy, who had pushed out a column of infantry considerably
to the rear of our line. This column was, in turn, forced
back to the position on the Shady Grove Road, which was
occupied by what was reported to be Hancock's corps.
Following up and crossing a small stream just below a mill
pond, we succeeded in reaching Waite's Shop, from whence
an attack was made on the enemy, and the entire force
which had crossed the Po was driven back with a loss of one
piece of artillery, which fell into our hands, and a considerable number in killed and wounded. This relieved us
from a very threatening danger, as the position the enemy
had attained would have enabled him to completely enfilade
Field's position, and get possession of the line of our communications to the rear, within a very short distance of which
he was, when met by the force which drove him back. In
this affair, Heth's division behaved very handsomely, all of
the brigades, (Cook's, Davis', Kirkland's, and Walker's,)
being engaged in the attack. General H. H. Walker had
the misfortune to receive a severe wound in the foot, which
rendered amputation necessary, but, otherwise, our loss was
slight. As soon as the road was cleared, Mahone's division
crossed the Po, but it was not practicable to pursue the affair
further, as the north bank of the stream at this point was
covered by a heavily entrenched line, with a number of
batteries, and night was approaching.

On the morning of the 11th, Heth was moved back to
Spottsylvania Court House, and Mahone was left to occupy
the position on the Shady Grove Road, from which the enemy
had been driven.*

My line on the right had been connected with Ewell's

---

* It will be seen, that after this affair, I held, for a time, both of General
Lee's flanks, which was rather an anomaly, but it could not be avoided, as we
had no reserves, and the two other corps, being immediately in front of the enemy
in line of battle, and almost constantly engaged, could not be moved without
great risk. It was absolutely necessary to occupy the position held on the left
by Mahone, to avoid a renewal of the danger from which we had escaped.

right, and covered the Fredericksburg Road, as also the road leading from Spottsylvannia Court House across the Ny into the road from Fredericksburg to Hanover Junction. Wilcox was on my left uniting with Ewell, and Heth joined him. The enemy had extended his lines across the Fredericksburg Road, but there was no fighting on this front on the 10th or 11th, except some artillery firing.

On the afternoon of the 11th, the enemy was demonstrating to our left, up the Po, as if to get possession of Shady Grove and the road from thence to Louisa Court House. General Hampton reported a column of infantry moving up the Po, and I was ordered by General Lee to take possession of Shady Grove, by light next morning, and hold it against the enemy. To aid in that purpose, two brigades of Wilcox's division, (Thomas' and Scales') were moved from the right, and Mahone was ordered to move before light to Shady Grove ; but during the night it was discovered that the movement to our left was a feint, and that there was a real movement of the enemy towards our right.

Before daybreak on the morning of the 12th, Wilcox's brigades were returned to him, and at dawn, Mahone's division was moved to the right, leaving Wright's brigade of that division to cover the crossing of the Po on Field's left. On this morning, the enemy made a very heavy attack on Ewell's front, and broke the line where it was occupied by Johnson's division. A portion of the attacking force swept along Johnson's line to Wilcox's left, and was checked by a prompt movement on the part of Brigadier General Lane, who was on that flank. As soon as the firing was heard, General Wilcox sent Thomas' and Scales' brigades to Lane's assistance, and they arrived just as Lane's brigade had repulsed this body of the enemy, and they pursued it for a short distance. As soon as Mahone's division arrived from the left, Perrin's and Harris' brigades of that division, and subsequently, McGowan's brigade of Wilcox's division were sent to General Ewell's assistance, and were carried into action under his orders. Brigadier General Perrin was killed, and Brigadier General McGowan severely wounded, while gallantly leading their respective brigades into action; and all the brigades sent to Ewell's assistance suffered severely.

Subsequently, on the same day, under orders from General Lee, Lane's brigade of Wilcox's division, and Mahone's own brigade (under Colonel Weisiger), were thrown to the front, for the purpose of moving to the left, and attacking the flank, of the column of the enemy which had broken Ewell's line, to relieve the pressure on him, and, if possible, recover the part of the line which had been lost. Lane's brigade commenced the movement and had not proceeded far, when it encountered and attacked, in a piece of woods in front of my line, the 9th corps, under Burnside, moving up to attack a salient on my front. Lane captured over three hundred prisoners, and three battle flags, and his attack on the enemy's flank, taking him by surprise, no doubt, contributed materially to his repulse. Mahone's brigade did not become seriously engaged. The attacking column which Lane encountered, got up to within a very short distance of a salient defended by Walker's brigade of Heth's division, under Colonel Mayo, before it was discovered, as there was a pine thicket in front, under cover of which the advance was made. A heavy fire of musketry from Walker's brigade, and Thomas' which was on its left, and a fire of artillery from a considerable number of guns on Heth's line, were opened with tremendous effect upon the attacking column, and it was driven back with heavy loss, leaving its dead in front of our works. This affair took place under the eye of General Lee himself. In the afternoon, another attempt was made to carry out the contemplated flank movement, with Mahone's brigade, and Cook's brigade of Heth's division, to be followed up by the other troops under my command; but it was discovered that the enemy had one or more entrenched lines in our front, to the fire from which our flanking column would have been exposed. Moreover, the ground between the lines was very rough, being full of rugged ravines and covered with thick pines and other growth; and it was thought advisable to desist from the attempt. The two brigades which were to have commenced the movement, were then thrown to the front on both sides of the Fredericksburg road, and, passing over two lines of breastworks, defended by a strong force of skirmishers, developed the existence of a third and much stronger line in rear, which would have afforded an almost insuperable obstacle to the proposed flank movement This closed the operations of the corps under my command on the memorable 12th of May.

Between that day and the 19th, there was no serious attack on my front, but much manœuvring by the enemy. General Mahone made two or three reconnoissances to the front, which disclosed the fact that the enemy was gradually moving to our right. In making one of them, he encountered a body of the enemy which had got possession of Gayle's house, on the left of the road leading from our right towards the Fredericksburg and Hanover Junction road, at which a portion of our cavalry, under Brigadier General Chambliss, had been previously posted, and drove it back across the Ny.* Another reconnoissance, handsomely made by Brigadier General Wright, who had been brought from the left, ascertained that a heavy force of the enemy was between the Ny and the Po, in front of my right, which was held by Mahone, and was along the road towards Hanover Junction. To meet this movement of the enemy, Fields' division was brought from the left and placed on my right.

On the 19th, General Ewell made a movement against the enemy's right, and to create a diversion in his favour, Thomas' brigade was thrown forward, and drove the enemy into his works in front of the salient, against which Burnside's attack had been made on the 12th, while the whole corps was held

---

* The Mattapony River, which, by its junction with the Pamunkey, forms York River, is formed by the confluence of four streams, called respectively, the "Mat," "Ta," "Po," and "Ny." The Ny is north and east of Spottsylvannia Court House, and behind it the enemy did most of his manœuvring in my front. It unites with the Po, a few miles to the east and south of Spottsylvannia Court House, and both streams are difficult to cross, except where there are bridges.

in readiness to co-operate with Ewell, should his attack prove successful ; but, as he was compelled to retire, Thomas was withdrawn.

Subsequently, the enemy retired from Heth's and Wilcox's fronts ; and, on the afternoon of the 21st, Wilcox was sent out on the road leading from Mahone's front across the Ny, with two of his brigades to feel the enemy, and found him still in force behind entrenched lines, and had a brisk engagement with that force.

While Wilcox was absent, an order was received by me, from General Lee, to turn over to General Hill the command of his corps, as he had reported for duty. I did so at once, and thus terminated my connection with this corps, which I had commanded during all the trying scenes around Spottsylvannia Court House. The officers and men of the corps had all behaved well, and contributed, in no little degree, to the result by which Grant was compelled to wait six days for reinforcements from Washington, before he could resume the offensive, or make another of his flank movements to get between General Lee's army and Richmond.

HANOVER JUNCTION.

OPERATIONS OF EARLY'S DIVISION.

The movement of the enemy to get between our army and Richmond had been discovered, and, on the afternoon of the 21st, Ewell's corps was put in motion towards Hanover Junction.* After turning over to General Hill, the command

---

*Hanover Junction is about 22 miles from Richmond, and is at the intersection of the Richmond Fredericksburg and Potomac railroad with the Central railroad from Richmond west, via Gordonsville and Staunton. It is on the direct road both from Spottsylvannia Court House and Fredericksburg to Richmond. The North Anna River is north of the Junction about two miles, and the South Anna about three miles south of it. These two streams unite south of east, and a few miles from the Junction, and form the Pamunkey River.

of his corps, I rode in the direction taken by Ewell's corps, and overtook it, a short time before day on the morning of the 22nd. Hoke's brigade, under Lieutenant Colonel Lewis, this day joined us from Petersburg, and an order was issued transferring Gordon's brigade, now under the command of Brigadier General Evans, to Johnson's division, which was placed under the command of General Gordon, who had been made a Major General. This left me in command of three brigades, to wit : Pegram's, Hoke's, and Johnston's, all of which were very much reduced in strength. My Adjutant General, Major Daniel, had been disabled for life by a wound received at the Wilderness, and my Inspector General, Major Samuel Hale, had been mortally wounded at Spottsylvannia Court House, on the 12th, while serving with the division and acting with great gallantry during the disorder which ensued after Ewell's line was broken. Both were serious losses to me.

On this day, (the 22nd), we moved to Hanover Junction, and, next day my division was posted on the extreme right, covering a ferry two or three miles below the railroad bridge across the North Anna. While at Hanover Junction my division was not engaged. At one time it was moved towards our left, for the purpose of supporting a part of the line on which an attack was expected, and moved back again without being required. It was, subsequently, placed temporarily on the left of the corps, relieving Rodes' division and a part of Fields' while the line was being remodelled, and then took position on the right again.

During the night of the 26th, the enemy again withdrew from our front.*

---

*At Hanover Junction General Lee was joined by Pickett's division of Longstreet's corps, and Breckinridge with two small brigades of infantry, and a battalion of artillery. These, with Hoke's brigade, were the first and only reinforcements received by General Lee since the opening of the campaign. Yet, Grant's immense army, notwithstanding the advantage gained by it on the 12th of May, had been so crippled, that it was compelled to wait six days at Spottsylvannia Court House for reinforcements from Washington, before it could resume the offensive. Breckinridge's infantry numbered less than 3000 muskets ; yet, Grant puts it at 15000, and he makes an absurd attempt to cast the whole

BATTLES OF COLD HARBOUR.

OPERATIONS OF EWELL'S CORPS.

On the 27th, the enemy having withdrawn to the north bank of the north Anna, and commenced another flank movement by moving down the north bank of the Pamunkey, Ewell's corps, now under my command, by reason of General Ewell's sickness, was moved across the South Anna over the bridge of the Central railroad, and by a place called "Merry Oaks," leaving Ashland on the Richmond Fredericksburg and Potomac railroad to the right, and bivouacked for the night at Hughes' cross road, the intersection of the road from Ashland to Atlee's station on the Central railroad with the road from the Merry Oaks to Richmond. Next morning I moved by Atlee's station to Hundley's corner, at the intersection of the road from Hanover Town, (the point at which Grant crossed the Pamunkey,) by Pole Green Church, to Richmond, with the road from Atlee's station, by Old Church in Hanover County, to the White House, on the Pamunkey. This is the point from which General Jackson commenced his famous attack on McClellan's flank and rear, in 1862, and it was very important that it should be occupied, as it intercepted Grant's direct march towards Richmond. All these movements were made under orders from General Lee.

My troops were placed in position, covering the road by Pole Creen Church, and also the road to Old Church, with my right resting near Beaver Dam Creek, a small stream running

---

blame for the failure of the campaign, so far, on Butler; to immolate whom he makes a digression in his account of the operations at Hanover Junction, and says: "The army sent to operate against Richmond having hermetically sealed itself up at Bermuda Hundreds, the enemy was enabled to bring the most, if not all the reinforcements brought from the south by Beauregard against the Army of the Potomac." He therefore determined to try another flank movement, and to get more reinforcements from the army at Bermuda Hundreds.

towards Mechanicsville and into the Chickahominy. Brigadier General Ramseur of Rodes' division, was this day
assigned to the command of my division. Ewell's corps, the
2nd of the Army of Northern Virginia, now numbered less
than 9,000 muskets for duty, its loss, on the 12th of May, having been very heavy.

On the 29th, the enemy having crossed the Tottopotomoy,
(a creek running just north of Pole Green church, and east-
ward to the Pamunkey,) appeared in my front on both roads,
and there was some skirmishing, but no heavy fighting.

On the afternoon of the 30th, in accordance with orders
from General Lee, I moved to the right across Beaver Dam,
to the road from Old Church to Mechanicsville, and thence
along that road towards Old Church, until we reached Bethesda
Church.   At this point the enemy was encountered, and his
troops which occupied the road, were driven by Rodes' division towards the road from Hundley's corner, which unites
with the road from Mechanicsville, east of Bethesda Church.
Pegram's brigade, under the command of Colonel Edward
Willis of the 12th Georgia regiment, was sent forward, with
one of Rodes' brigades on its right, to feel the enemy, and
ascertain his strength ; but, meeting with a heavy force behind
breastworks, it was compelled to retire, with the loss of some
valuable officers and men, and among them were Colonel
Willis, mortally wounded, and Colonel Terrill of the 13th
Virginia regiment, and Lieutenant Colonel Watkins of the
52nd Virginia regiment, killed.   This movement showed that
the enemy was moving to our right flank, and at night, I withdrew a short distance on the Mechanicsville road, covering it
with my force.   When I made the movement from Hundley's
corner, my position at that place was occupied by a part of
Longstreet's corps, under Anderson.

On the next morning, my troops were placed in position on
the east side of Beaver Dam across the road to Mechanicsville,
but Rodes was subsequently moved to the west side of the
creek.

Grant's movement to our right, towards Cold Harbour, was

continued on the 31st, and the 1st of June, and corresponding movements were made by General Lee to meet him, my command retaining its position with a heavy force in its front.

On the 2nd, all the troops on my left, except Heth's division of Hill's corps, had moved to the right, and, in the afternoon of that day, Rodes' division moved forward, along the road from Hundley's corner towards Old Church, and drove the enemy from his entrenchments, now occupied with heavy skirmish lines, and forced back his left towards Bethesda Church, where there was a heavy force. Gordon swung round so as to keep pace with Rodes, and Heth co-operated, following Rodes and taking position on his left flank. In this movement there was some heavy fighting and several hundred prisoners were taken by us. Brigadier-General Doles, a gallant officer of Rodes' division, was killed, but otherwise our loss was not severe.

On the next day (the 3rd.), when Grant made an attack at Cold Harbour in which he suffered very heavily, there were repeated attacks on Rodes' and Heth's fronts, those on Cook's brigade, of Heth's division, being especially heavy, but all of them were repulsed. There was also heavy skirmishing on Gordon's front. During the day, Heth's left was threatened by the enemy's cavalry, but it was kept off by Walker's brigade under Colonel Fry, which covered that flank, and also repulsed an effort of the enemy's infantry to get to our rear. As it was necessary that Heth's division should join its corps on the right, and my flank in this position was very much exposed, I withdrew at the close of the day to the line previously occupied, and next morning Heth moved to the right.

My right now connected with the left of Longstreet's corps under General Anderson. The enemy subsequently evacuated his position at Bethesda Church and his lines in my front, and, having no opposing force to keep my troops in their lines, I made two efforts to attack the enemy on his right flank and rear. The first was made on the 6th, when I crossed the Matadaquean (a small stream, running through wide swamps in the enemy's rear), and got in rear of his right flank, driving in his skirmishers until we came to a swamp, which could be crossed only on a narrow causeway defended by an entrenched line with artillery. General Anderson was to have co-operated with me, by moving down the other side of the Matadaquean, but the division sent for that purpose did not reach the position from which I started until near night, and I was therefore compelled to retire as my position was too much exposed.

On the next day (the 7th.), a reconnoissance made in front of Anderson's line, showed that the greater part of it was uncovered, and, in accordance with instructions from General Lee, I moved in front of, and between it and the Matadaquean, until my progress was arrested by a ravine and swamp which prevented any further advance, but a number of pieces of artillery were opened upon the enemy's position in flank and reverse, so as to favour a movement from Anderson's front, which had been ordered but was not made; and at night I retired from this position to the rear of our lines.

Since the fighting at the Wilderness, Grant had made it an invariable practice to cover his front, flank, and rear, with a perfect network of entrenchments, and all his movements were made under cover of such works. It was therefore very difficult to get at him.

On the 11th., my command was moved to the rear of Hill's line, near Gaines' Mill; and, on the 12th., I received orders to move, with the 2nd. corps, to the Shenadoah Valley, to meet Hunter. This, therefore, closed my connection with the campaign from the Rapidan to James River.

When I moved, on the morning of the 13th., Grant had already put his army in motion to join Butler, on James River, a position which he could have reached, from his camps on the north of the Rapidan, by railroad and transports, without the loss of a man. In attempting to force his way by land, he had already lost, in killed and wounded, more men than were in General Lee's entire army; and he was compelled to give up, in despair, the attempt to reach Richmond in that way.[*]

* Grant, in describing his movement from Spottsylvania Court House to Han-over Junction, says: " But the enemy again having the shorter line, and being in

possession of the main roads, was enabled to reach the North-Anna in advance of us, and took position behind it." And, when he speaks of his final determination to join Butler, he says: "After the Battle of the Wilderness. it was evident that the enemy deemed it of the first importance to run no risk with the army he then had. He acted purely on the defensive, behind breastworks, or, feebly on the offensive, immediately in front of them, and where, in case of repulse, he could retire behind them. Without a greater sacrifice of life than I was willing to make, all could not be accomplished that I designed north of Richmond."

Mr. Secretary Stanton, with a keenness of strategic acumen which is altogether unparalleled, says : "Forty three days of desperate fighting or marching, by day and night. forced back the rebel army from the Rapidan to their entrenchments around Richmond, and carried the Army of the Potomac to the south side of James River. The strength of the enemy's force when the campaign opened, or the extent of his loss, is not known to this Department. Any inequality between Lee's army and the Army of the Potomac, was fully compensated by the advantage of position."

We are left in the dark whether it was the desperate fighting or the desperate marching which did all this ; but, however that may be, it was a wonderful achievement, especially when it is considered that the Army of the Potomac might have been carried to the south side of James River by transports, and Lee's army thereby forced back to the entrenchments around Richmond, without the " Forty-three days of desperate fighting or marching, by day and night," and without the loss of men sustained by Grant. There are some who think Stanton is slyly making fun of Grant; but, if he is not, and is in dead earnest, the question naturally arises, in the mind of one not as gifted as the Federal Secretary of War: How happened it that, if Lee was being constantly forced back, for forty-three days, over a distance of more than eighty miles, he always had the shorter line, and posses-ion of the main roads, and got the advantage of position, and had time to fortify it?

I happen to know that General Lee always had the grea'est anxiety to strike at Grant, in the open field ; and I should like to know when it was that the latter operated on the defensive, or offensive either, except behind, or immediately in front of, far better entrenchments than General Lee's army, with its limited means, was able to make An inspection of the battle-fields, from the Rapidan to the James, will show that Grant's army did a vast deal more digging than General Lee's.

The truth is, that the one commander was a great captain, and perfect master of his art, while the other had none of the requisites of a great captain, but merely possessed the most ordinary brute courage, and had the control of unlimited numbers and means. Yet, it is claimed that Grant fights and writes better than Alexander, and Hannibal, and Cæsar, and Napoleon, and all the rest; and when, in the exercise of his great powers of composition, he turns the batteries of his rhetoric on Butler, I say, in his own classic language, " Go in ! " You can't hit him a lick amiss ! I cannot, however, but be amused at the effort to make Butler the scape-goat ; and cannot help thinking that Grant ought to have known, beforehand, that he (Butler) was unfit to make war, except on defenceless women and children, and that the trophies valued by him were not those won at the cannon's mouth.

Grant, in his report, has enunciated the leading principles of his strategy, and he is certainly entitled to the credit of having practised them, if not to the merit of originality. They were : " First, to use the greatest number of troops practicable against the armed force of the enemy ; " and, " Second, to hammer continuously against the armed force of the enemy, and his resources, until, by mere attrition, if by nothing else, there should be nothing left to him but an equal submission, with the loyal section of our common country, to the constitution and laws of the land." (Alas ! what has become of the constitution and laws ?) This latter principle was more concisely and forcibly expressed by Mr. Lincoln, when he declared his purpose to " keep a-pegging." The plain English of the whole idea was to continue raising troops, and to oppose them, in overwhelming numbers, to the Confederate Army, until the latter should wear itself out whipping them, when a newly-recruited army might " go in and win." And, this was actually what took place in regard to General Lee's army.

Grant having established his fame as a writer, as well as fighter, I presume he will give the world the benefit of his ideas, and publish a work on strategy, which I would suggest ought to be called " The Lincoln-Grant or Pegging-Hammer Art of War."

He has made some observations, in his report, about the advantages of interior lines of communication, supposed to be possessed by the Confederate commanders, which are more specious than sound. The Mississippi River divided the Confederacy into two parts, and the immense naval power of the enemy enabled him to render communication across that river, after the loss of New Orleans and Memphis, always difficult, and finally to get entire possession of it. On the eastern side of it, the railroad communications were barely sufficient for the transportation of supplies, and the transportation of troops over them was always tedious and difficult. The Ohio River, in the West, and the Potomac, in the East, with the mountains of Western Virginia, rendered it impossible for an invading army to march into the enemy's country, except at one or two fords on the Potomac, just east of the Blue Ridge, and two or three fords above Harper's Ferry. The possession of the seas, and the blockade of our ports, as well as the possession of the Mississippi, the Ohio, and Potomac Rivers, with the Baltimore and Ohio Railroad, and the railroads through Pennsylvania, Ohio, Indiana, Illinois, Kentucky, and Tennessee, enabled the enemy to transport troops, from the most remote points, with more ease and rapidity than they could be transported over the railroads under the control of the Confederate Government, all of which were in bad condition. The enemy, therefore, in fact had all the advantages of interior lines ; that is, rapidity of communication and concentration, with the advantage, also, of unrestricted communication with all the world, which his naval power gave him.

CAMPAIGN IN MARYLAND

AND

THE VALLEY OF VIRGINIA.

~~~~~~~~~~~~~~~~

INTRODUCTION.

The Valley of Virginia, in its largest sense, embraces all that country lying between the Blue Ridge and Alleghany Mountains, which unite at its south-western end.

The Shenandoah Valley, which is a part of the Valley of Virginia, embraces the Counties of Augusta, Rockingham, Shenandoah, Page, Warren, Clarke, Frederick, Jefferson and Berkeley. This Valley is bounded on the north by the Potomac, on the south by the County of Rockbridge, on the east by the Blue Ridge, and on the west by the Great North Mountain and its ranges.

The Shenandoah River is composed of two branches, called, respectively, the " North Fork " and the " South Fork," which unite near Front Royal in Warren County. The North Fork rises in the Great North Mountain, and runs eastwardly to within a short distance of New Market in Shenandoah County, and thence north-east by Mount Jackson to Strasburg, where it turns east to Front Royal. The South Fork is formed by the union of North River, Middle River, and South River. North River and Middle River, running from the west, unite near Mount Meridian in Augusta County. South River rises in the south-eastern part of Augusta, and runs by Waynesboro, along the western base of the Blue Ridge, to Port Republic in Rockingham, where it unites with the stream formed by the junction of the North and Middle Rivers, a few miles above. From Port Republic, the South Fork of the Shenandoah runs north-east, through the eastern border of Rockingham and the county of Page, to Front Royal in Warren County.

The North Fork and South Fork are separated by the Massanutten Mountain, which is connected with no other mountain, but terminates abruptly at both ends. Its northern end is washed at its base, just below Strasburg, by the North Fork. Its southern end terminates near the road between Harrisonburg and Conrad's Store on the South Fork, at which latter place the road through Swift Run Gap in the Blue Ridge crosses that stream. Two valleys are thus formed, the one on the North Fork being called "The Main Valley," and the other on the South Fork, and embracing the County of Page and part of the County of Warren, being usually known by the name of "The Luray Valley." The Luray Valley unites with the Main Valley at both ends of the mountain. There is a good road across Massanutten Mountain, from one valley to the other, through a gap near New-Market. South of this gap there is no road across the mountain, and north of it the roads are very rugged and not practicable for the march of a large army with its trains. At the northern or lower end of Massanutten Mountain, and between two branches of it, is a valley called "Powell's Fort Valley" or more commonly "The Fort." This valley is accessible only by the very rugged roads over the mountain which have been mentioned, and through a ravine at its lower end. From its isolated position, it was not the theatre of military operations of any consequence, but merely furnished a refuge for deserters, stragglers, and fugitives from the battle fields.

From Front Royal, the Shenandoah River runs along the western base of the Blue Ridge to Harper's Ferry, where it unites with the Potomac, which here bursts through the mountains. The mountain in extension of the range of the Blue Ridge from this point through Maryland and Pennsylvania is called "South Mountain."

Strictly speaking, the County of Berkeley and the greater

part of Frederick are not in the Valley of the Shenandoah. The Opequon, rising south-west of Winchester, and crossing the Valley Pike four or five miles south of that place, turns to the north and empties into the Potomac some distance above its junction with the Shenandoah ; the greater part of Frederick and nearly the whole of Berkeley being on the western side of the Opequon.

Little North Mountain, called in the lower valley " North Mountain," runs north-east, through the western portions of Shenandoah, Frederick and Berkeley Counties, to the Potomac. At its northern end, where it is called North Mountain, it separates the waters of the Opequon from those of Back Creek.

Cedar Creek rises in Shenandoah County, west of Little North Mountain, and running north-east along its western base, passes through that mountain, four or five miles from Strasburg, and, then making a circuit, empties into the North Fork of the Shenandoah, about two miles below Strasburg.

The Baltimore and Ohio Railroad crosses the Potomac at Harper's Ferry, and, passing through Martinsburg in Berkeley County, crosses Back Creek near its mouth, runs up the Potomac, crossing the South Branch of that river near its mouth, and then the North Branch to Cumberland in Maryland. From this place it runs into Virginia again and, passing through North Western Virginia, strikes the Ohio River by two stems terminating at Wheeling and Parkersburg respectively.

There is a railroad from Harper's Ferry to Winchester, called " The Winchester and Potomac Railroad," and also one from Manassas Junction on the Orange and Alexandria Railroad, through Manassas Gap in the Blue Ridge, by Front Royal and Strasburg, to Mount Jackson, called " The Manassas Gap Railroad ;" but both of these roads were torn up and rendered unserviceable in the year 1862, under the orders of General Jackson.

From Staunton in Augusta County, there is a fine macadamized road called " The Valley Pike," running through Mount Sydney, Mount Crawford, Harrisonburg, New Market,

Mount Jackson, Edinburg, Woodstock, Strasburg, Middletown, Newtown, Bartonsville and Kernstown to Winchester in Frederick County, and crossing Middle River seven miles from Staunton, North River at Mount Crawford eighteen miles from Staunton, the North Fork of the Shenandoah at Mount Jackson, Cedar Creek between Strasburg and Middletown, and the Opequon at Bartonsville, four or five miles from Winchester. There is also another road west of the Valley Pike, connecting these several villages, called the " Back Road," and, in some places, another road between the Valley Pike and the Back Road, which is called the " Middle Road."

From Winchester there is a macadamized road, via Martinsburg, to Williamsport on the Potomac in Maryland, and another, via Berryville in Clarke County, and Charlestown in Jefferson County, to Harper's Ferry. There is also a good pike from Winchester to Front Royal, which crosses both forks of the Shenandoah just above their junction ; and from Front Royal there are good roads up the Luray Valley, and by the way of Conrad's Store and Port Republic, to Harrisonburg and Staunton.

From Staunton, south, there are good roads passing through Lexington, in Rockbridge County, and Buchanan, in Bottetourte County, to several points on the Virginia and Tennessee Railroad ; and others direct from Staunton and Lexington to Lynchburg.

The Central Railroad, from Richmond, passes through the Blue-Ridge, with a tunnel, at Rock-fish Gap, and runs through Waynesboro and Staunton, westwardly, to Jackson's River, which is one of the head-streams of James River.

This description of the country is given in order to render the following narrative intelligible without too much repetition.

In the spring of 1864, before the opening of the campaign, the lower Shenandoah Valley was held by the Federal troops, under Major-General Sigel, with his head-quarters at Winchester, while the upper Valley was held by Brigadier-General Imboden, of the Confederate Army, with one brigade of cavalry, or mounted infantry, and a battery of artillery. When the campaign opened, Sigel moved up the Valley, and Major-General Breckenridge moved from South-Western Virginia, with two brigades of infantry and a battalion of artillery, to meet him. Breckenridge, having united his forces with Imboden's, met and defeated Sigel, at New Market, on the 15th day of May, driving him back towards Winchester. Breckenridge then crossed the Blue Ridge, and joined General Lee, at Hanover Junction, with his two brigades of infantry and the battalion of artillery. Subsequently, the Federal General Hunter organized another and larger force than Sigel's, and moved up the Valley; and, on the 5th day of June, defeated Brigadier-General William E. Jones, at Piedmont, between Port Republic and Staunton—Jones' force being composed of a very small body of infantry, and a cavalry force which had been brought from South-Western Virginia, after Breckenridge's departure from the Valley. Jones was killed, and the remnant of his force, under Brigadier-General Vaughan, fell back to Waynesboro. Hunter's force then united with another column which had moved from Lewisburg, in Western Virginia, under the Federal General Crook. As soon as information was received of Jones' defeat and death, Breckenridge was sent back to the Valley, with the force he had brought with him.

MARCH TO LYNCHBURG, AND PURSUIT OF HUNTER.

On the 12th of June, while the 2nd Corps (Ewell's) of the Army of Northern Virginia was lying near Gaines' Mill, in rear of Hill's line at Cold Harbour, I received verbal orders from General Lee, to hold the corps, with two of the battalions of artillery attached to it, in readiness to move to the Shenandoah Valley. Nelson's and Braxton's battalions were selected, and Brigadier-General Long was ordered to accompany me as Chief of Artillery. After dark, on the same day, written instructions were given me by General Lee, by which I was directed to move, with the force designated, at 3 o'clock next morning, for the Valley, by the way of Louisa C.H. and Charlottesville, and through Brown's or Swift Run Gap in the Blue Ridge, as I might find most advisable; to strike Hunter's force in the rear, and, if possible, destroy it; then to move down the valley, cross the Potomac near Leesburg in Loudon County, or at or above Harper's Ferry, as I might find most practicable, and threaten Washington City. I was further directed to communicate with General Breckenridge, who would co-operate with me in the attack on Hunter, and the expedition into Maryland.

At this time the railroad and telegraph lines between Charlottesville and Lynchburg had been cut by a cavalry force from Hunter's army; and those between Richmond and Charlottesville had been cut by Sheridan's cavalry, from Grant's army; so that there was no communication with Breckenridge. Hunter was supposed to be at Staunton with his whole force, and Breckenridge was supposed to be at Waynesboro, or Rock-fish Gap. If such had been the case, the route designated by General Lee would have carried me into the Valley in Hunter's rear.

The 2nd Corps now numbered a little over 8,000 muskets

for duty. It had been on active and arduous service in the field for forty days, and had been engaged in all the great battles from the Wilderness to Cold Harbour, sustaining very heavy losses at Spottsylvania C.H., where it lost nearly an entire division, including its commander, Major-General Johnson, who was made prisoner. Of the Brigadier-Generals with it at the commencement of the campaign, only one remained in command of his brigade. Two (Gordon and Ramseur) had been made Major-Generals; one (G. H. Steuart) had been captured; four (Pegram, Hays, J. A. Walker, and R. D. Johnston) had been severely wounded; and four (Stafford, J. M. Jones, Daniel, and Doles) had been killed in action. Constant exposure to the weather, a limited supply of provisions, and two weeks' service in the swamps north of the Chickahominy had told on the health of the men. Divisions were not stronger than brigades ought to have been, nor brigades than regiments.

On the morning of the 13th, at two o'clock, we commenced the march; and, on the 16th, arrived at the Rivanna River, near Charlottesville, having marched over eighty miles in four days.*

From Louisa C.H. I had sent a dispatch to Gordonsville, to be forwarded, by telegraph, to Breckenridge; and, on my arrival at Charlottesville, on the 16th, to which place I rode in advance of the troops, I received a telegram from him,

---

* On the 15th., we passed over the ground, near Trevillian's depot, on which Hampton and Sheridan had fought, on the 11th. and 12th. Hampton had defeated Sheridan, and was then in pursuit of him. Grant claims, in his report, that, on the 11th., Sheridan drove our cavalry "from the field, in complete rout;" and says, when he advanced towards Gordonsville, on the 12th., "he found the enemy reinforced by infantry, behind well-constructed rifle-pits, about five miles from the latter place, and too strong to successfully assault."

This is as thoroughly a fancy sketch as can well be manufactured. There was not an infantry soldier in arms nearer the scene of action than with General Lee's army, near Cold Harbour; and, the "well-constructed rifle-pits" were nothing more than rails put up in the manner in which cavalry were accustomed to arrange them to prevent a charge. Sheridan mistook some of Hampton's cavalry, dismounted and fighting on foot, for infantry; and the statement was made to cover his defeat.

dated at Lynchburg, informing me that Hunter was then in Bedford County, about twenty miles from that place, and moving on it.

The railroad and telegraph between Charlottesville and Lynchburg had been, fortunately, but slightly injured by the enemy's cavalry, and had been repaired. The distance between the two places was sixty miles, and there were no trains at Charlottesville, except one which belonged to the Central road, and was about starting for Waynesboro. I ordered this to be detained, and immediately directed, by telegram, all the trains of the two roads to be sent to me with all dispatch, for the purpose of transporting my troops to Lynchburg. The trains were not in readiness to take the troops on board until sunrise on the morning of the 17th, and then only enough were furnished to transport about half of my infantry. Ramseur's division, one brigade of Gordon's division, and part of another were put on the trains, as soon as they were ready, and started for Lynchburg. Rodes' division, and the residue of Gordon's, were ordered to move along the railroad, to meet the trains on their return. The artillery and waggon-trains had been started on the ordinary roads, at daylight.

I accompanied Ramseur's division, going on the front train, but the road and rolling stock were in such bad condition that I did not reach Lynchburg until about one o'clock in the afternoon, and the other trains were much later. I found General Breckinridge in bed, suffering from an injury received by the fall of a horse killed under him in action near Cold Harbour. He had moved from Rockfish Gap to Lynchburg by a forced march, as soon as Hunter's movement towards that place was discovered. When I showed him my instructions, he very readily and cordially offered to co-operate with me, and serve under my command.

Hunter's advance fron Staunton had been impeded by a brigade of cavalry, under Brigadier General McCausland, which had been managed with great skill, and kept in his front all the way, and he was reported to be then advancing on the old stone turnpike from Liberty in Bedford County by New London, and watched by Imboden with a small force of cavalry.

As General Breckenridge was unable to go out, at his request, General D. H. Hill, who happened to be in town, had made arrangements for the defence of the city, with such troops as were at hand. Brigadier General Hays, who was an invalid from a wound received at Spottsylvannia Court House, had tendered his services and also aided in making arrangements for the defence. I rode out with General Hill to examine the line selected by him, and make a reconnoissance of the country in front. Slight works had been hastily thrown up on College Hill, covering the turnpike and Forest roads from Liberty, which were manned by Breckenridge's infantry and the dismounted cavalry of the command which had been with Jones at Piedmont. The reserves, invalids from the hospitals, and the cadets from the Military Institute at Lexington, occupied other parts of the line. An inspection satisfied me that, while this arrangement was the best which could be made under the circumstances in which General Hill found himself, yet it would leave the town exposed to the fire of the enemy's artillery, should he advance to the attack, and I therefore determined to meet the enemy with my troops in front.

We found Imboden about four miles out on the turnpike, near an old Quaker church, to which position he had been gradually forced back by the enemy's infantry. My troops, as they arrived, had been ordered in front of the works to bivouac, and I immediately sent orders for them to move out on this road, and two brigades of Ramseur's division arrived just in time to be thrown across the road, at a redoubt about two miles from the city, as Imboden's command was driven back by vastly superior numbers. These brigades, with two pieces of artillery in the redoubt, arrested the progress of the enemy, and Ramseur's other brigade, and the part of Gordon's division which had arrived, took position on the same line. The enemy opened a heavy fire of artillery on us, but, as night soon came on, he went into camp in our front.*

On my arrival at Lynchburg, orders had been given for the immediate return of the trains for the rest of my infantry, and I expected it to arrive by the morning of the 18th, but it did not get to Lynchburg until late in the afternoon of that day. Hunter's force was considerably larger than mine would have been, had it all been up, and as it was of the utmost consequence to the army at Richmond that he should not get into Lynchburg, I did not feel justified in attacking him until I could do so with a fair prospect of success. I contented myself therefore with acting on the defensive on the 18th, throwing Breckenridge's infantry and a part of his artillery on the front line, while that adopted by General Hill was occupied by the dismounted cavalry and the irregular troops. During the day, there was artillery firing and skirmishing along the line, and, in the afternoon, an attack was made on our line, to the right of the turnpike, which was handsomely repulsed with considerable loss to the enemy. A demonstration of the enemy's cavalry on the Forest road, was checked by part of Breckenridge's infantry under Wharton, and Mc-Causland's cavalry.

On the arrival of the cars from Richmond this day, Major Generals Elzey and Ransom reported for duty, the former to command the infantry and dismounted cavalry of Brecken-

---

* Hunter's delay in advancing from Staunton had been most remarkable, and can only be accounted for by the fact, that indulgence in petty acts of malignity and outrage upon private citizens was more congenial to his nature than bold operations in the field. He had defeated Jones' small force at Piedmont about ten miles from Staunton, on the 5th, and united with Crook on the 8th, yet he did not arrive in front of Lynchburg until near night on the 17th. The route from Staunton to Lynchburg by which he moved, which was by Lexington, Buchanan, the Peaks of Otter, and Liberty, is about one hundred miles in distance. It is true McCausland had delayed his progress by keeping constantly in his front, but an energetic advance would have brushed away McCausland's small force, and Lynchburg, with all its manufacturing establishments and stores, would have fallen before assistance arrived. A subsequent passage over the greater part of the same route showed how Hunter had been employed.

ridge's command, and the latter to command the cavalry. The mounted cavalry consisted of the remnants of several brigades divided into two commands, one under Imboden, and the other under McCausland. It was badly mounted and armed, and its efficiency much impaired by the defeat at Piedmont, and the arduous service it had recently gone through.

As soon as the remainder of my infantry arrived by the railroad, though none of my artillery had gotten up, arrangements were made for attacking Hunter at daylight on the 19th, but, sometime after midnight, it was discovered that he was moving, though it was not known whether he was retreating, or moving so as to attack Lynchburg on the south where it was vulnerable, or to attempt to join Grant on the south side of James River. Pursuit could not, therefore, be made at once, as a mistake, if either of the last two objects had been contemplated, would have been fatal. At light, however, the pursuit commenced, the 2nd Corps moving along the turnpike, over which it was discovered Hunter was retreating, and Elzey's command on the right, along the Forest road, while Ransom was ordered to move on the right of Elzey, with McCausland's cavalry, and endeavour to strike the enemy at Liberty or the Peaks of Otter. Imboden, who was on the road from Lynchburg to Campbell Court House, to watch a body of the enemy's cavalry, which had moved in that direction the day before, was to have moved on the left towards Liberty, but orders did not reach him in time. The enemy's rear was overtaken at Liberty, twenty-five miles from Lynchburg, just before night, and driven through that place, after a brisk skirmish, by Ramseur's division. The days march on the old turnpike, which was very rough, had been terrible. McCausland had taken the wrong road and did not reach Liberty until after the enemy had been driven through the town.

It was here ascertained that Hunter had not retreated on the route by the Peaks of Otter, over which he had advanced, but had taken the road to Buford's depot, at the foot of the Blue Ridge, which would enable him to go either by Salem, Fincastle, or Buchanan. Ransom was, therefore, ordered to

take the route, next day, by the Peaks of Otter, and endeavour
to intercept the enemy should he move by Buchanan or Fincastle.   The pursuit was resumed early on the morning of
the 20th, and on our arrival in sight of Buford's, the enemy's
rear guard was seen going into the mountain on the road
towards Salem.   As this left the road to Buchanan open, my
aide, Lieutenaat Pitzer, was sent across the mountain to that
place, with orders to Ransom to move for Salem.   Lieutenant
Pitzer was also instructed to ride all night and send directions,
by courier from Fincastle, and telegraph from Salem, to have
the road through the mountains to Lewisburg and South
Western Virginia blockaded.   The enemy was pursued into
the mountains at Buford's Gap, but he had taken possession
of the crest of the Blue Ridge, and put batteries in position
commanding a gorge, through which the road passes, where
it was impossible for a regiment to move in line.   I had
endeavoured to ascertain if there was not another way across the
mountain by which I could get around the enemy, but all the
men, except the old ones, had gotten out of the way, and the
latter, as well as the women and children, were in such a
state of distress and alarm, that no reliable information could
be obtained from them.   We tried to throw forces up the
sides of the mountains to get at the enemy, but they were so
rugged that night came on before anything could be accomplished, and we had to desist, though not until a very late
hour in the night.

By a mistake of the messenger, who was sent with orders
to General Rodes, who was to be in the lead next morning,
there was some delay in his movement on the 21st, but the
pursuit was resumed very shortly after sun-rise.   At the Big
Lick, it was ascertained that the enemy had turned off from
Salem towards Lewisburg, on a road which passes through
the mountains at a narrow pass called the " Hanging Rock,"
and my column was immediately turned towards that point,
but on arriving there it was ascertained that the enemy's rear
guard had passed through the gorge.   McCausland had struck
his column at this point and captured ten pieces of artillery,

some waggons, and a number of prisoners; but, the enemy having brought up a heavy force, McCausland was compelled to fall back, carrying off, however, the prisoners, and a part of the artillery, and disabling the rest so that it could not be removed. As the enemy had got into the mountains, where nothing useful could be accomplished by pursuit, I did not deem it proper to continue it farther. A great part of my command had had nothing to eat for the last two days, except a little bacon which was obtained at Liberty. The cooking utensils were in the trains, and the effort to have bread baked at Lynchburg had failed. Neither the waggon trains, nor the artillery of the 2nd corps, were up, and I knew that the country, through which Hunter's route led for forty or fifty miles, was, for the most part, a desolate mountain region; and that his troops were taking everything in the way of provisions and forage which they could lay their hands on. My field officers, except those of Breckenridge's command, were on foot, as their horses could not be transported on the trains from Charlottesville. I had seen our soldiers endure a great deal, but there was a limit to the endurance even of Confederate soldiers. A stern chase with infantry is a very difficult one, and Hunter's men were marching for their lives, his disabled being carried in his provision train which was now empty. My cavalry was not strong enough to accomplish anything of importance, and a further pursuit could only have resulted in disaster to my command from want of provisions and forage.

I was glad to see Hunter take the route to Lewisburg, as I knew he could not stop short of the Kanawha River, and he was, therefore, disposed of for some time. Had he moved to South Western Virginia, he would have done us incalculable mischief, as there were no troops of any consequence in that quarter, but plenty of supplies at that time. I should, therefore, have been compelled to follow him.*

---

* Grant, in his report says: "General Hunter, owing to a want of ammunition to give battle, retired from before the place" (Lynchburg). This is a little

My command had marched sixty miles, in the three days pursuit, over very rough roads, and that part of it from the Army of Northern Virginia had had no rest since leaving Gaines' Mill. I determined, therefore, to rest on the 22nd, so as to enable the waggons and artillery to get up, and prepare the men for the long march before them. Imboden had come up, following on the road through Salem after the enemy, and the cavalry was sent through Fincastle, to watch the enemy and annoy him as he passed through the mountains towards Lewisburg, and also ascertain whether he would endeavour to get into the valley towards Lexington or Staunton.

---

remarkable, as it appears that this expedition had been long contemplated and was one of the prominent features of the campaign of 1864. Sheridan, with his cavalry, was to have united with Hunter at Lynchburg, and the two together were to have destroyed General Lee's communications and depots of supplies, and then have joined Grant. Can it be believed that Hunter set out on so important an expedition with an insufficient supply of ammunition? He had only fought the battle of Piedmont with a part of his force, and it was not a very severe one, as Jones' force was a small one and composed mostly of cavalry. Crook's column not being there was not engaged. Had Sheridan defeated Hampton at Trevillian's, he would have reached Lynchburg after destroying the railroad on the way, and I could not have reached there in time to do any good. But Hampton defeated Sheridan, and the latter saw "infantry" "too strong to successfully assault." Had Hunter moved on Lynchburg with energy, that place would have fallen before it was possible for me to get there. But he tarried on the way for purposes which will hereafter appear, and when he reached there, his heart failed him and he was afraid to fight an inferior force, and then there was discovered, "A want of ammunition to give battle."

MARCH DOWN THE VALLEY, AND OPERATIONS IN THE LOWER VALLEY AND MARYLAND.

At Lynchburg, I had received a telegram from General Lee, directing me, after disposing of Hunter, either to return to his army or carry out the original plan, as I might deem most expedient under the circumstances in which I found myself. After the pursuit had ceased, I received another dispatch from him, submitting it to my judgment whether the condition of my troops would permit the expedition across the Potomac to be carried out, and I determined to take the responsibility of continuing it. On the 23rd, the march was resumed and we reached Buchanan that night, where we struck again the route over which Hunter had advanced.* Ransom's cavalry moved

---

* The scenes on Hunter's route from Lynchburg had been truly heart-rending. Houses had been burned, and helpless women and children left without shelter. The country had been stripped of provisions and many families left without a morsel to eat. Furniture and bedding had been cut to peices, and old men and women and children robbed of all the clothing they had except that on their backs. Ladies trunks had been rifled and their dresses torn to peices in mere wantonness. Even the negro girls had lost their little finery. We now had renewed evidences of the outrages committed by Hunter's orders in burning and plundering private houses. We saw the ruins of a number of houses to which the torch had been applied by his orders. At Lexington he had burned the Military Institute, with all of its contents, including its library and scientific apparatus; and Washington College had been plundered and the statue of Washington stolen. The residence of Ex-Governor Letcher at that place had been burned by orders, and but a few minutes given Mrs. Letcher and her family to leave the house. In the same county a most excellent christian gentleman, a Mr. Creigh, had been hung, because, on a former occasion, he had killed a straggling and marauding Federal soldier while in the act of insulting and outraging the ladies of his family. These are but some of the outarges committed by Hunter or his orders, and I will not insult the memory of the ancient barbarians of the North by calling them "acts of Vandalism." If those old barbarians were savage and cruel, they at least had the manliness and daring of rude soldiers, with occasional traits of magnanimity. Hunter's deeds were those of a malignant and cowardly fanatic, who was better qualified to make war upon helpless women and children than upon armed soldiers. The time consumed in the perpretration of those deeds, was the salvation of Lynchburg, with its stores, foundries, and factories, which were so necessary to our army at Richmond.

by Clifton Forge, through the western part of Rockbridge, to
keep a lookout for Hunter and ascertain if he should attempt
to get into the Valley again.

On the 26th, I reached Staunton in advance of the troops,
and the latter came up next day, which was spent in reducing
transportation and getting provisions from Waynesboro, to
which point they had been sent over the railroad. Some of
the guns and a number of the horses belonging to the artillery
were now unfit for service, and the best of each were selected,
and about a battalion taken from Breckenridge's artillery,
under Lt. Col. King, to accompany us, in addition to the two
battalions brought with the 2nd Corps. The rest were left
behind with a portion of the officers and men in charge of
them. The dismounted cavalry had been permitted to send
for their horses which had been recruiting, and Col. Bradley T.
Johnson, who had joined me at this place with a battalion of
Maryland Cavalry, was assigned to the command of Jones'
brigade, with the temporary rank of Brigadier General, that
brigade having been reorganized and the two Maryland battalions attached to it. General Breckenridge had accompanied
us from Lynchburg, and, to give him a command commensu-
rate with his proper one, and at the same time enable me to control the cavalry more readily, Gordon's division of infantry
was assigned to his command in addition to the one under
Elzey, and Ransom, in charge of the cavalry, was ordered to
report to me directly. Major General Elzey was relieved
from duty at his own request, and the division under him
was left under the temporary command of Brigadier General
Vaughan.

The official reports at this place showed about two thousand
mounted men for duty in the cavalry, which was composed of
four small brigades, to wit: Imboden's, McCausland's, Jackson's, and Jones' (now Johnson's). Vaughan's had not been
mounted but the horses had been sent for from South-western
Virginia. The official reports of the infantry showed 10,000
muskets for duty, including Vaughan's dismounted cavalry.
Nearly, if not quite half of the company officers and men were

barefooted or nearly so, and a dispatch had been sent from Salem by courier, and Lynchburg by telegraph, to Richmond, requesting shoes to be sent to Staunton, but they had not arrived.

Another telegram was received here from Gen. Lee, stating that the circumstances under which my original orders were given had changed, and again submitting it to my judgment, in the altered state of things, whether the movement down the Valley and across the Potomac should be made. The accession to my command from Breckenridge's forces had not been as great as General Lee supposed it would be, on account of the disorganization consequent on Jones' defeat at Piedmont, and the subsequent rapid movement to Lynchburg from Rock-fish Gap, but I determined to carry out the original design at all hazards, and telegraphed to General Lee my purpose to continue the movement.

The march was resumed on the 28th with five days rations in the waggons and two days in haversacks, empty waggons being left to bring the shoes when they arrived. Imboden was sent through Brock's Gap in the Great North Mountain to the Valley of the South Branch of the Potomac, with his brigade of cavalry and a battery of horse artillery, to destroy the rail-road bridge over that stream and all the bridges on the Baltimore and Ohio rail-road from that point to Martinsburg. The telegraph line was repaired to New-Market as we marched down the Valley, and communications kept up with that point by signal stations. On the 2nd of July we reached Winchester,*

---

* On this day we passed through Newtown where several houses, including that of a Methodist minister, had been burned by Hunter's orders, because a part of Mosby's command had attacked a train of supplies for Sigel's force, at this place. The original order was to burn the whole town, but the officer sent to execute it had revolted at the cruel mandate of his superior, and another had been sent who but partially executed it, after having forced the people to take an oath of allegiance to the United States to save their houses. Mosby's battalion, though called " guerillas" by the enemy, was a regular organization in the Confederate Army, and was merely serving on detached duty under General Lee's orders. The attack on the train was an act of legitimate warfare, and the order to burn Newtown, and the burning of the houses mentioned were most wanton, cruel, unjustifiable, and cowardly.

and I here received a dispatch from General Lee, directing me to remain in the lower Valley until everything was in readiness to cross the Potomac, and to destroy the Baltimore and Ohio railroad and the Chesapeake and Ohio Canal as far as possible. This was in accordance with my previous determination, and its policy was obvious. My provisions were nearly exhausted and if I had moved through Loudon, it would have been necessary for me to halt and thresh wheat and have it ground, as neither bread nor flour could be otherwise obtained ; which would have caused much greater delay than was required on the other route, where we could take provisions from the enemy. Moreover unless the Baltimore and Ohio railroad was torn up, the enemy would have been able to move troops from the West over that road to Washington.

On the night of the 2nd, McCausland was sent across North Mountain, to move down Back Creek, and burn the railroad bridge at its mouth, and then to move by North Mountain depot to Haynesville, on the road from Martinsburg to Williamsport ; and, early on the morning of the 3rd, Bradley Johnson was sent by Smithfield and Leetown, to cross the railroad at Kearneysville, east of Martinsburg, and unite with McCausland, at Haynesville, so as to cut off the retreat of Sigel, who was at Martinsburg with a considerable force. Breckenridge moved, on the same morning, direct for Martinsburg, with his command preceded by Gilmor's battalion of cavalry, while I moved, with Rodes' and Ramseur's divisions, over the route taken by Johnson, to Leetown. On the approach of Breckenridge, Sigel, after very slight skirmishing, evacuated Martinsburg, leaving behind considerable stores, which fell into our hands. McCausland burned the bridge over Back Creek, captured the guard at North Mountain depot, and succeeded in reaching Haynesville ; but Johnson encountered a force at Leetown, under Mulligan, which, after hard fighting, he drove across the railroad, when, Sigel having united with Mulligan, Johnson's command was forced back, just before night, on Rodes' and Ramseur's divisions, which had arrived at Leetown, after a march of twenty-four miles. It was too late, and these divisions were too much exhausted, to go after the enemy ; and, during the night, Sigel retreated across the Potomac, at Shepherdstown, to Maryland Heights.

On the 4th, Shepherdstown was occupied by a part of Ransom's cavalry. Rodes' and Ramseur's divisions moved to Harper's Ferry, and the enemy was driven from Bolivar Heights, and the Village of Bolivar, to an inner line of works under the cover of the guns from Maryland Heights. Breckenridge, after burning the railroad bridges at Martinsburg, and across the Opequon, moved to Duffield's depot, five miles from Harper's Ferry, destroying the road as he moved. During the night of the 4th, the enemy evacuated Harper's Ferry, burning the railroad and pontoon bridges across the Potomac.

It was not possible to occupy the town of Harper's Ferry, except with skirmishers, as it was thoroughly commanded by the heavy guns on Maryland Heights ; and the 5th was spent by Rodes' and Ramseur's divisions in demonstrating at that place. In the afternoon, Breckenridge's command crossed the river at Shepherdstown, and Gordon's division was advanced over the Antietam, towards Maryland Heights. At night, considerable stores, which had been abandoned at Harper's Ferry, were secured ; and, before day, Rodes' and Ramseur's divisions moved to Shepherdstown, and crossed the Potomac early on the 6th, Lewis' brigade, of Ramseur's division, being left to occupy Harper's Ferry with skirmishers.

On this day (the 6th) Gordon's division advanced towards Maryland Heights, and drove the enemy into his works. Working parties were employed in destroying the aqueduct of the canal over the Antietam, and the locks and canalboats.

On the 7th, Rodes moved through Rohersville, on the road to Crampton's Gap in South Mountain, and skirmished with a small force of the enemy, while Breckenridge demonstrated against Maryland Heights, with Gordon's division, supported by his other division, now under Brigadier-General Echols, who had reported for duty.

While these operations were going on, McCausland had occupied Hagerstown, and levied a contribution of $20,000, and Boonsboro had been occupied by Johnson's cavalry. On the 6th I received a letter from General Lee, by special courier, informing me that, on the 12th, an effort would be made to release the prisoners at Point Lookout, and directing me to take steps to unite them with my command, if the attempt was successful; but I was not informed of the manner in which the attempt would be made—General Lee stating that he was not, himself, advised of the particulars.

My desire had been to manœuvre the enemy out of Maryland Heights, so as to enable me to move directly from Harper's Ferry for Washington; but he had taken refuge in his strongly-fortified works, and, as they could not be approached without great difficulty, and an attempt to carry them by assault would have resulted in greater loss than the advantage to be gained would justify, I determined to move through the gaps of South Mountain to the north of the Heights. On the 7th, the greater portion of the cavalry was sent across the mountain, in the direction of Frederick; and, that night, the expected shoes having arrived and been distributed, orders were given for a general move next morning; and an officer (Lieut.-Col. Goodwin, of a Louisiana Regiment) was ordered back to Winchester, with a small guard, to collect the stragglers at that place, and prevent them from following.

Imboden had reached the railroad, at the South Branch of the Potomac, and partially destroyed the bridge, but had not succeeded in dislodging the guard from the b ock-house at that place. He had been taken sick, and very little had been accomplished by the expedition; and his brigade, now under the command of Colonel George H. Smith, had returned.

Early on the morning of the 8th, the whole force moved; Rodes, through Crampton's Gap, to Jefferson; Breckenridge, through Fox's Gap; and Ramseur, with the trains, through

Boonsboro Gap, followed by Lewis' brigade, which had started from Harper's Ferry the night before, after burning the trestle-work on the railroad, and the stores which had not been brought off. Breckenridge and Ramseur encamped near Middletown, and Rodes near Jefferson. Ransom had occupied Catoctan Mountain, between Middletown and Frederick, with his cavalry, and had skirmished heavily with a body of the enemy at the latter place. McCausland was ordered to move to the right, in the afternoon, and the next day cut the telegraph and railroad between Maryland Heights and Washington and Baltimore—cross the Monocacy, and, if possible, occupy the railroad bridge over that stream, at the Junction near Frederick.

Early on the 9th, Johnson, with his brigade of cavalry, and a battery of horse artillery, moved to the north of Frederick, with orders to strike the railroads from Baltimore to Harrisburg and Philadelphia, burn the bridges over the Gunpowder, also to cut the railroad between Washington and Baltimore, and threaten the latter place ; and then to move towards Point Lookout, for the purpose of releasing the prisoners, if we should succeed in getting into Washington. The other troops also moved forward towards Monocacy Junction, and Ramseur's division passed through Frederick, driving a force of skirmishers before it.

BATTLE OF MONOCACY.

The enemy, in considerable force under General Lew Wallace, was found strongly posted on the eastern bank of the Monocacy near the Junction, with an earthwork and two block houses commanding both the railroad bridge and the bridge on the Georgetown pike. Ramseur's division was deployed in front of the enemy, after driving his skirmishers across the river, and several batteries were put in position, when a sharp artillery fire opened from both sides. Rodes' division had come up from Jefferson and was placed on Ramseur's left, covering the roads from Baltimore and the crossings of the Monocacy above the Junction Breckenridge's command, with the trains, was in the rear between Frederick and the Junction, while the residue of the cavalry was watching a force of the enemy's cavalry which had followed from Maryland Heights. The enemy's position was too strong, and the difficulties of crossing the Monocacy under fire too great, to attack in front without greater loss than I was willing to incur. I therefore made an examination in person to find a point at which the river could be crossed, so as to take the enemy in flank. While I was engaged in making this examination to my right, I discovered McCausland in the act of crossing the river with his brigade. As soon as he crossed, he dismounted his men, and advanced rapidly against the enemy's left flank, which he threw into confusion, and he came very near capturing a battery of artillery, but the enemy concentrated on him, and he was gradually forced back obstinately contesting the ground. McCausland's movement, which was very brilliantly executed, solved the problem for me, and, as soon as I discovered it, orders were sent to Breckenridge to move up rapidly with Gordon's division to McCausland's assistance, and to follow up his attack. This division crossed at the same place, and Gordon was ordered to move forward and strike the enemy on his left flank, and drive him from the position commanding the crossings in Ramseur's front, so as to enable the latter to cross. This movement was executed under the personal superintendence of General Breckenridge, and, while Ramseur skirmished with the enemy in front, the attack was made by Gordon in gallant style, and, with the aid of several pieces of King's artillery which had been crossed over, and Nelson's artillery from the opposite side, he threw the enemy into great confusion and forced him from his position. Ramseur immediately crossed on the railroad bridge and pursued the enemy's flying forces, and Rodes crossed on the left and joined in the pursuit. Echol's division which had been left to guard the trains, was ordered up during the engagement, but was not needed. The pursuit was soon discontinued, as Wallace's entire force had taken the road towards Baltimore, and I did not want prisoners. Wallace's force I estimated at 8000 or 10,000 men, and it was ascertained that one division of the 6th corps (Rickett's) from Grant's army, was in the fight. Between 600 and 700 unwounded prisoners fell into our hands, and the enemy's loss in killed and wounded was very heavy. Our loss in killed and wounded was about 700, and among them were brigadier General Evans wounded, and Colonel Lamar of the 61st Georgia regiment, Lieutenant-Colonel Tavener, of the 17th Virginia cavalry, and Lieutenant Hobson, of Nelson's artillery, killed. The action closed about sunset, and we had marched fourteen miles before it commenced. All the troops and trains were crossed over the Monocacy that night, so as to resume the march early next day. Such of our wounded as could not be moved in ambulances or otherwise, were sent to the hospitals at Frederick under charge of competent medical officers, and our dead were buried. During the operations at Monocacy, a contribution of $200,000 in money was levied on the city of Frederick, and some needed supplies were obtained.

OPERATIONS IN FRONT OF WASHINGTON, AND RECROSSING THE POTOMAC.

On the 10th, the march was resumed at daylight, and we bivouacked four miles from Rockville, on the Georgetown pike, having marched twenty miles. Ramseur's division, which had remained behind for a short time to protect a working party engaged in destroying the railroad bridge, was detained for a time in driving off the party of cavalry which had been following from Maryland Heights, and did not get up until one o'clock at night.   McCausland, moving in front on this day, drove a body of the enemy's cavalry before him, and had quite a brisk engagement at Rockville, where he encamped after defeating and driving off the enemy.

We moved at daylight on the 11th; McCausland moving on the Georgetown pike, while the infantry, preceeded by Imboden's cavalry under Colonel Smith, turned to the left at Rockville, so as to reach the 7th street pike which runs by Silver Spring into Washington.   Jackson's cavalry moved on the left flank.   The previous day had been very warm, and the roads were exceedingly dusty, as there had been no rain for several weeks.   The heat during the night had been very oppressive, and but little rest had been obtained.   This day was an exceedingly hot one, and there was no air stirring. While marching, the men were enveloped in a suffocating cloud of dust, and many of them fell by the way from exhaustion.   Our progress was therefore very much impeded, but I pushed on as rapidly as possible, hoping to get into the fortifications around Washington before they could be manned. Smith drove a small body of cavalry before him into the works on the 7th street pike, and dismounted his men and deployed them as skirmishers.   I rode ahead of the infantry, and arrived in sight of Fort Stevens on this road a short time after noon, when I discovered that the works were but feebly manned.

Rodes, whose division was in front, was immediately ordered to bring it into line as rapidly as possible, throw out skirmishers, and move into the works if he could.   My whole column was then moving by flank, which was the only practicable mode of marching on the road we were on, and before Rodes' division could be brought up, we saw a cloud of dust in the rear of the works towards Washington, and soon a column of the enemy filed into them on the right and left, and skirmishers were thrown out in front, while an artillery fire was opened on us from a number of batteries.   This defeated our hopes of getting possession of the works by surprise, and it became necessary to reconnoitre.

Rode's skirmishers were thrown to the front, driving those of the enemy to the cover of the works, and we proceeded to examine the fortifications in order to ascertain if it was practicable to carry them by assault. They were found to be exceedingly strong, and consisted of what appeared to be enclosed forts for heavy artillery, with a tier of lower works in front of each pierced for an immense number of guns, the whole being connected by curtains with ditches in front, and strengthened by palisades and abattis. The timber had been felled within cannon range all around and left on the ground, making a formidable obstacle, and every possible approach was raked by artillery. On the right was Rock Creek, running through a deep ravine which had been rendered impassable by the felling of the timber on each side, and beyond were the works on the Georgetown pike which had been reported to be the strongest of all. On the left, as far as the eye could reach, the works appeared to be of the same impregnable character. The position was naturally strong for defence, and the examination shewed, what might have been expected, that every appliance of science and unlimited means had been used to render the fortifications around Washington as strong as possible. This reconnoissance consumed the balance of the day.

The rapid marching, which had broken down a number of the men who were barefooted or weakened by previous exposure, and had been left in the Valley and directed to be collected at Winchester, and the losses in killed and wounded at Harper's Ferry, Maryland Heights, and Monocacy, had reduced my infantry to about 8,000 muskets. Of those remaining, a very large number were greatly exhausted by the last two days marching, some having fallen by sunstroke, and I was satisfied, when we arrived in front of the fortifications, that not more than one third of my force could have been carried into action. I had about forty pieces of field artillery, of which the largest were 12 pounder Napoleons, besides a few pieces of horse artillery with the cavalry. McCausland reported the works on the Georgetown pike too strongly manned for him to assault. We could not move to the right or the left without its being discovered from a signal station on the top of the " Soldiers' Home," which overlooked the country, and the enemy would have been enabled to move in his works to meet us.   Under the circumstances, to have rushed my men blindly against the fortifications, without understanding the state of things, would have been worse than folly.   If we had any friends in Washington, none of them came out to give us information, and this satisfied me that the place was not undefended.   I knew that troops had arrived from Grant's army, for prisoners had been captured from Rickett's division of the 6th corps at Monocacy.   From Sharpsburg I had sent a message to Mosby, by one of his men, requesting him to cross the Potomac below Harper's Ferry, cut the railroad and telegraph, and endeavour to find out the condition of things in Washington, but he had not crossed the river and I had received no information from him. A northern paper, which was obtained, gave the information that Hunter, after moving up the Ohio River in steamboats, was passing over the Baltimore and Ohio railroad, and I knew that he would be at Harper's Ferry soon, as Imboden had done very little damage to the road west of Martinsburg. After dark on the 11th, I held a consultation with Major Generals Breckenridge, Rodes, Gordon, and Ramseur, in which I stated to them the danger of remaining where we were, and the necessity of doing something immediately, as the probability was that the passes of the South Mountain and the fords of the upper Potomac would soon be closed against us. After interchanging views with them, being very reluctant to abandon the project of capturing Washington, I determined to make an assault on the enemy's works at daylight next morning, unless some imformation should be received before that time showing its impracticability,and so informed those officers. During the night a dispatch was received from Gen. Bradley Johnson from near Baltimore, informing me that he had received information, from a reliable source, that two corps had arrived from Gen. Grant's army, and that his whole army was probably in motion.   This caused me to delay the attack until

I could examine the works again, and, as soon as it was light enough to see, I rode to the front and found the parapets lined with troops. I had, therefore, reluctantly, to give up all hopes of capturing Washington, after I had arrived in sight of the dome of the Capitol, and given the Federal authorities a terrible fright.

Grant in his report says, in regard to the condition of things when I moved towards Washington : " The garrisons of Baltimore and Washington were at this time made up of heavy artillery regiments, hundred days men, and detachments from the invalid corps." And, in regard to the force of Wallace at Monocacy, he says ; " His force was not sufficient to ensure success, but he fought the enemy nevertheless, and although it resulted in a defeat to our arms, yet it detained the enemy and thereby served to enable Gen. Wright to reach Washington with two divisions of the 6th Corps, and the advance of the 19th Corps, before him." Stanton says in his report : " Here (at Washington) they (we) were met by troops from the Army of the Potomac, consisting of the 6th Corps under General Wright, a part of the 8th Corps under General Gilmore, and a part of the 19th Corps, just arrived from New Orleans under General Emory." Taking Grant's statement of the troops which had arrived from his army as the most reliable, they were sufficient to hold the works against my troops, at least until others could arrive. But, in addition to those which had already arrived, there were the detachments from the invalid corps, called, I believe, the " Veteran Reserves " (of which I was informed there were about 5,000), the heavy artillery regiments, the hundred days' men, and, I suppose, the part of the 8th corps mentioned by Stanton. To all these may be added the local troops, or militia, and the government employees. Some of the northern papers stated that, between Saturday and Monday, I could have entered the city ; but on Saturday I was fighting at Monocacy, thirty-five miles from Washington, a force which I could not leave in my rear ; and, after disposing of that force and moving as rapidly as it was possible for me to move, I did not arrive in front of the fortifications until after noon on Monday, and then my troops were exhausted, and it required time to bring them up into line.   I had then made a march, over the circuitous route by Charlottesville, Lynchburg, and Salem, down the Valley, and through the passes of the South Mountain, which, notwithstanding the delays in dealing with Hunter's, Sigel's, and Wallace's forces, is, for its length and rapidity, I believe, without a parallel in this or any other modern war—the unopposed marauding excursion of the freebooter Sherman through Georgia, not excepted.   My small force had been thrown up to the very walls of the Federal Capital, north of a river which could not be forded at any point within 40 miles, and with a heavy force and the South Mountain in my rear—the passes through which mountain could be held by a small number of troops.   A glance at the map, when it is recollected that the Potomac is a wide river, and navigable to Washington for the largest vessels, will cause the intelligent reader to wonder, not why I failed to take Washington, but why I had the audacity to approach it as I did, with the small force under my command.   It was supposed by some, who were not informed of the facts, that I delayed in the lower Valley longer than was necessary ; but, an examination of the foregoing narrative will show that not one moment was spent in idleness, but that every one was employed in making some arrangement, or removing some difficulty in my way, which it was necessary to make or remove, so as to enable me to advance with a prospect of success.   I could not move across the Potomac and through the passes of the South Mountain, with any safety, until Sigel was driven from, or safely housed in, the fortifications at Maryland Heights.

After abandoning the idea of capturing Washington, I determined to remain in front of the fortifications during the 12th, and retire at night, as I was satisfied that to remain longer would cause the loss of my entire force.

Johnson had burned the bridges over the Gunpowder, on the Harrisburg and Philadelphia roads, threatened Baltimore, and started for Point Lookout, but I sent an order for him to return. The attempt to release the prisoners of which I was informed by General Lee, was not made, as the enemy had received notice of it in some way. Major Harry Gilmor, who burned the bridge over the Gunpowder on the Philadelphia road, captured Major General Franklin on a train at that point, but he was permitted to escape, either by the carelessness or exhaustion of the guard placed over him, before I was informed of the capture.

On the afternoon of the 12th, a heavy reconnoitring force was sent out by the enemy, which, after severe skirmishing, was driven back by Rodes' division with but slight loss to us. About dark we commenced retiring and did so without molestation.* Passing through Rockville and Poolsville, we crossed the Potomac at White's Ford, above Leesburg in Loudon County, on the morning of the 14th, bringing off the prisoners captured at Monocacy and everything else in safety. There was some skirmishing in the rear between our cavalry and that of the enemy which was following, and, on the afternoon of the 14th, there was some artillery firing by the enemy, across the river, at our cavalry which was watching the fords. Besides the money levied in Hagerstown and Frederick, which was subsequently very useful in obtaining supplies, we brought off quite a large number of beef cattle, and the cavalry obtained a number of horses, some being also procured for the artillery.†

---

* Grant says : "On the 12th, a reconnoissance was thrown out in front of Fort Stevens to ascertain the enemy's position and force. A severe skirmish ensued, in which we lost 280 in killed and wounded. The enemy's loss was probably greater. He commenced retiring during the night." In regard to the same affair, Stanton says ; " By these troops (Wright's, Gilmore's, and Emory's) the enemy was was driven back from Washington and retreated hastily to Virginia, pursued by our forces under General Wright." Grant's statement is correct, with the exception of the estimate he places on our loss. Comment on Stanton's is unneccessary when it is compared with that of Grant.

† On the night of the 12th, the house of Postmaster General Blair near Silver Spring was burned, and it was assumed by the enemy that it was burned by my orders. The fact is, that I had nothing to do with it, and do not yet know how the burning occurred. Though I believed that retaliation was fully justified by the previous acts of the enemy, yet I did not wish to incur the risk of any license

RETURN TO THE VALLEY, AND OPERATIONS THERE.

We rested, on the 14th. and 15th., near Leesburg; and, on the morning of the 16th., resumed the march to the Valley, through Sincker's Gap in the Blue Ridge. Hunter had arrived at Harper's Ferry, and united with Sigel, and the whole force had moved from that place, under Crook, to Hillsboro, in Loudon, and a body of cavalry from it made a dash on our train, as we were moving towards the Valley, and succeeded in setting fire to a few waggons, but was soon driven off by troops from Rodes' and Ramseur's divisions, and one piece of artillery was captured from the enemy.

On the morning of the 17th., we crossed the Shenandoah, at Snicker's or Castleman's Ferry, and took position near Berryville—Breckenridge covering the ford at the ferry, and

---

on the part of my troops, and it was obviously impolitic to set the house on fire when we were retiring, as it amounted to notice of our movement. Some of my officers thought the burning was done by some person in the neighborhood, who took advantage of our presence to commit the act with impunity. It may have been occasioned by a shell from the enemy's guns, some of which went in that direction late in the day, or it may have been the act of some of my men; and a number of them had abundant provocation for the act, in the sight of their own devastated homes as they marched down the Valley on Hunter's track. In retaliation for the burning of this house, two Federal gunboats with a body of soldiers on board were sent up the Rappahannock River, on which there was not a Confederate soldier, to burn the house of the widow of the brother of the Hon. James A. Seddon, the Confederate Secretary of War, and she and her little children were turned out of doors, and the house with all its contents consigned to the flames. A card was left, signed by Butler or his order, stating that the house was burned in retaliation for the burning of the Hon. Montgomery Blair's house. This retaliation upon a widowed lady and her orphan children, by a combined military and naval expedition, was worthy of the agent selected, and the cause in which he was engaged. But, though it was very congenial to his nature, I do not regard Butler as alone responsible for this act. The odium of it should attach to his superiors Lincoln and Grant, he being the favourite of the former, and the subordinate of the latter, and at that time, serving under his immediate orders.

the river above and below, and Rodes' and Ramseur's divisions the roads from Harper's Ferry.

On the 18th, the enemy, having moved through Snicker's Gap, appeared on the banks of the Shenandoah, and there was some skirmishing. In the afternoon, a heavy column of his infantry made a dash at Parker's Ford, one mile below the ferry, and crossed over, after driving back the picket of one hundred men at that point. Breckenridge moved Gordon's and Echol's divisions to the front, and held the enemy in check, while Rodes' division was brought up from the left, and attacked and drove him across the river, with heavy loss, and in great confusion.

On the 19th, the enemy's main body still occupied the eastern bank of the Shenandoah, and smaller columns moved up and down the river, to effect a crossing. Imboden, with his own and McCausland's cavalry, resisted and repulsed one of these columns, which attempted to cross at Berry's Ferry, with considerable loss to the enemy. The horses of Vaughan's cavalry having been brought from South-western Virginia, his small force had been now mounted. On this day I received information that a column under Averill was moving from Martinsburg towards Winchester, and, as the position I held near Berryville left my trains exposed to expeditions in the rear from Martinsburg and Harper's Ferry, I determined to concentrate my force near Strasburg, so as to enable me to put the trains in safety, and then move out and attack the enemy. This movement was commenced on the night of the 19th ; Ramseur's division, with a battery of artillery, being sent to Winchester, to cover that place against Averill, while the stores, and the sick and wounded were being removed, and the other divisions moving through Millwood and White Post to the Valley Pike at Newtown and Middletown.

Vaughan's and Jackson's cavalry had been watching Averill, and, on the afternoon of the 20th., it was reported to General Ramseur, by General Vaughan, that Averill was at Stephenson's depot, with an inferior force, which could be captured, and Ramseur moved out from Winchester to attack him ; but, relying on the accuracy of the information he had received, General Ramseur did not take the proper precautions in advancing, and his division, while moving by the flank, was suddenly met by a larger force, under Averill, advancing in line of battle, and the result was that Ramseur's force was thrown into confusion, and compelled to retire, with the loss of four pieces of artillery, and a number in killled and wounded—Brigadier-Generals Lewis and Lilly being among the wounded, and Col. Board, of the 58th Virginia Regiment, among the killed. Colonel Jackson made a vigorous charge with his cavalry, which enabled Ramseur to rally his men, restore order, and arrest the progress of Averill before he reached Winchester. The error committed, on this occasion, by this most gallant officer, was nobly retrieved in the subsequent part of the campaign. I received, at Newtown, the news of Ramseur's misfortune, and immediately moved to his assistance with Rodes' division ; but, on arriving at Winchester, I found that the enemy, after being checked, had fallen back a short distance ; and, as another and much larger column was moving through Berryville, I did not go after Averill, but moved the whole command to Newtown—the stores, and such of the wounded and sick as could be transported, having been gotten off.

On the 21st., my whole infantry force was concentrated near Middletown ; and, on the 22nd., it was moved across Cedar Creek, towards Strasburg, and so posted as to cover all the roads from the direction of Winchester.

A report having been sent to me, from Mt. Jackson, that a force of the enemy was moving from the Valley of the South Branch of the Potomac to that place, Imboden was sent to ascertain its truth, and it proved to be false. We rested on the 23rd., while waiting to ascertain the movements of the enemy, and during the day a report was received from the cavalry in front, that a large portion of the force sent after us from Washington, was returning, and that Crook and Averill had united, and were at Kernstown, near Winchester.

BATTLE OF KERNSTOWN.

On the reception of the foregoing information, I determined to attack the enemy at once ; and, early on the morning of the 24th., my whole force was put in motion for Winchester. The enemy, under Crook, consisting of the " Army of West Virginia," and including Hunter's and Sigel's forces, and Averill's cavalry, was found in position at Kernstown, on the same ground occupied by Shields, at the time of General Jackson's fight with him, on the 22nd of March, 1862. Ramseur's division was sent to the left, at Bartonsville, to get around the enemy's right flank, while the other divisions moved along the Valley Pike, and formed on each side of it. Ransom's cavalry was ordered to move in two columns ; one on the right, along the road from Front Royal to Winchester ; and the other on the left, and west of Winchester, so as to unite in rear of the latter place, and cut off the enemy's retreat. After the enemy's skirmishers were driven in, it was discovered that his left flank, extending through Kernstown, was exposed, and General Breckenridge was ordered to move Echol's division, now under Brig.-Gen. Wharton, under cover of some ravines on our right, and attack that flank. This movement, which was made under Gen. Breckenridge's personal superintendence, was handsomely executed, and the attacking division struck the enemy's left flank in open ground, doubling it up and throwing his whole line into great confusion. The other divisions then advanced, and the rout of the enemy became complete. He was pursued, by the infantry and artillery, through and beyond Winchester; and the pursuit was continued by Rodes' division to Stephenson's depot, six miles from Winchester—this division then having marched twenty-seven miles from its position west of Strasburg. The cavalry had not been moved according to my orders ; and the enemy, having the advantage of an open country and a wide macadamized road, was enabled to make

his escape with his artillery and most of his waggons. General Ransom had been in very bad health since he reported
to me at Lynchburg, and unable to take the active command
in the field ; and all my operations had been impeded for the
want of an efficient and energetic cavalry commander. I
think, if I had had one on this occasion, the greater part of
the enemy's force would have been captured or destroyed, for
the rout was thorough. Our loss, in this action, was very
light. The enemy's loss in killed and wounded was severe,
and two or three hundred prisoners fell into our hands ; and,
among them, Colonel Mulligan, in command of a division,
mortally wounded. The infantry was too much exhausted to
continue the pursuit on the 25th., and only moved to Bunker
Hill, twelve miles from Winchester. The pursuit was continued by our cavalry, and the enemy's rear-guard of cavalry
was encountered at Martinsburg ; but, after slight skirmishing, it evacuated the place. The whole defeated force crossed
the Potomac, and took refuge at Maryland Heights and Harper's Ferry. The road from Winchester, via Martinsburg, to
Williamsport, was strewed with debris of the rapid retreat—
twelve caissons and seventy-two waggons having been abandoned, and most of them burned *

EXPEDITION INTO MARYLAND AND PENNSYL-
VANIA—BURNING OF CHAMBERSBURG.

On the 26th we moved to Martinsburg, the cavalry going to
the Potomac. The 27th and 28th were employed in destroyng
the railroad, it having been repaired since we passed over it

---

* Grant in his report entirely ignores this battle, in which the enemy's forces
were superior to mine, and merely says :—" About the 25th, it became evident
that the enemy was again advancing upon Maryland and Pennsylvania, and
the 6th corps which was at Washington, was ordered back to the vicinity of
Harper's Ferry."

at the beginning of the month. While at Martinsburg, it was ascertained, beyond all doubt, that Hunter had been again indulging in his favourite mode of warfare, and that, after his return to the Valley, while we were near Washington, among other outrages, the private residences of Mr. Andrew Hunter, a member of the Virginia Senate, Mr. Alexander R. Boteler, an ex-member of the Confederate Congress as well as of the United States Congress, and Edmund I. Lee, a distant relative of General Lee, all in Jefferson County, with their contents, had been burned by his orders, only time enough being given for the ladies to get out of the houses. A number of towns in the South, as well as private country houses, had been burned by the Federal troops, and the accounts had been heralded forth in some of the Northern papers in terms of exultation, and gloated over by their readers, while they were received with apathy by others. I now came to the conclusion that we had stood this mode of warfare long enough, and that it was time to open the eyes of the people of the North to its enormity, by an example in the way of retaliation. I did not select the cases mentioned, as having more merit or greater claims for retaliation than others, but because they had occurred within the limits of the country covered by my command, and were brought more immediately to my attention.*

The town of Chambersburg in Pennsylvania was selected

---

* I had often seen delicate ladies, who had been plundered, insulted, and rendered desolate by the acts of our most atrocious enemies, and while they did not call for it, yet, in the anguished expressions of their features while narrating their misfortunes, there was a mute appeal to every manly sentiment of my bosom for retribution, which I could no longer withstand. On my passage through the lower Valley into Maryland, a lady had said to me, with tears in her eyes, " Our lot is a hard one and we see no peace, but there are a few green spots in our lives, and they are, when the Confederate soldiers come along and we can do something for them." May God defend and bless those noble women of the Valley, who so often ministered to the wounded, sick, and dying Confederate soldiers, and gave their last morsel of bread to the hungry! They bore with heroic courage, the privations, sufferings, persecutions, and dangers, to which the war which was constantly waged in their midst exposed them, and upon no portion of the Southern people did the disasters which finally befell our army and country, fall with more crushing effect than upon them.

as the one on which retaliation should be made, and McCausland was ordered to proceed, with his brigade and that of Johnson and a battery of artillery, to that place, and demand of the municipal authorities the sum of $100,000 in gold, or $500,000 in United States currency, as a compensation for the destruction of the houses named and their contents ; and, in default of payment, to lay the town in ashes, in retaliation for the burning of those houses and others in Virginia, as well as for the towns which had been burned in other Southern States. A written demand to that effect was sent to the municipal authorities, and they were informed what would be the result of a failure or refusal to comply with it. I desired to give the people of Chambersburg an opportunity of saving their town, by making compensation for part of the injury done, and hoped that the payment of such a sum would have the desired effect, and open the eyes of the people of other towns at the North, to the necessity of urging upon their government the adoption of a different policy. McCausland was also directed to proceed from Chambersburg towards Cumberland in Maryland, and levy contributions in money upon that and other towns able to bear them, and if possible destroy the machinery at the coal pits near Cumberland, and the machine shops, depots, and bridges on the Baltimore and Ohio railroad as far as practicable.

On the 29th, McCausland crossed the Potomac near Clear Spring, above Williamsport, and I moved with Rodes' and Ramseur's divisions and Vaughan's cavalry to the latter place, while Imboden demonstrated with his and Jackson's cavalry towards Harper's Ferry, in order to withdraw attention from McCausland. Breckenridge remained at Martinsburg and continued the destruction of the railroad. Vaughan drove a force of cavalry from Williamsport, and went into Hagerstown, where he captured and destroyed a train of cars loaded with supplies. One of Rodes' brigades was crossed over at Williamsport and subsequently withdrawn. On the 30th, McCausland being well under way, I moved back to Martinsburg, and on the 31st the whole infantry force was moved to Bunker Hill, where we remained on the 1st, 2nd, and 3rd of August.

On the 4th, in order to enable McCausland to retire from Pennsylvania and Maryland, and to keep Hunter, who had been reinforced by the 6th and 19th corps, and had been oscillating between Harper's Ferry and Monocacy Junction, in a state of uncertainty, I again moved to the Potomac with the infantry and Vaughan's and Jackson's cavalry, while Imboden demonstrated towards Harper's Ferry. On the 5th Rodes' and Ramseur's divisions crossed at Williamsport and took position near St. James' College, and Vaughan's cavalry went into Hagerstown. Breckenbridge, with his command, and Jackson's cavalry, crossed at Shepherdstown, and took position at Sharpsburg. This position is in full view from Maryland Heights, and a cavalry force was sent out by the enemy to reconnoitre, which, after skirmishing with Jackson's cavalry, was driven off by the sharpshooters of Gordon's division. On the 6th, the whole force recrossed the Potomac at Williamsport, and moved towards Martinsburg; and on the 7th we returned to Bunker Hill.*

---

* While at Sharpsburg on this occasion, I rode over the ground on which the battle of Sharpsburg, or Antietam as it is called by the enemy, was fought, and I was surprised to see how few traces remained of that great battle. In the woods at the famous Dunkard or Tunker Church, where, from personal observation at the battle, I expected to find the trees terribly broken and battered, a stranger would find difficulty in identifying the marks of the bullets and shells.

I will take occasion here to say that the public, North or South, has never known how small was the force with which General Lee fought that battle. McClellan's estimate is very wide of the mark. From personal observation and conversation with other officers engaged, including General Lee himself, I am satisfied that the latter was not able to carry 30,000 men into action. The exhaustion of our men, in the battles around Richmond, the subsequent battles near Manassas, and on the march to Maryland, when they were for days without anything to eat except green corn, was so great that the straggling was frightful before we crossed the Potomac. As an instance of our weakness, and a reminiscence worthy of being recorded, which was brought very forcibly to my mind while riding over the ground, I will state the following facts: In the early part of the day, all of General Jackson's troops on the field except my brigade (A. P. Hill had not then arrived from Harper's Ferry) were driven from the field in great disorder, and Hood had taken their place with his division. My brigade, which was on the extreme left supporting some artillery with which Stuart was operating, and had not been engaged, was sent for by Gen. Jackson and posted in the left of the woods at the Dunkard Church. Hood was also

On the 30th of July McCausland reached Chambersburg, and made the demand as directed, reading to such of the authorities as presented themselves the paper sent by me. The demand was not complied with, the people stating that they were not afraid of having their town burned, and that a Federal force was approaching. The policy pursued by our army on former occasions had been so lenient, that they did not suppose the threat was in earnest this time, and they hoped for speedy relief. McCausland, however, proceeded to carry out his orders, and the greater part of the town was laid in ashes.* He then moved in the direction of Cumberland, but, on approaching that town, he found it defended by a force under Kelly too strong for him to attack, and he withdrew towards Hampshire County in Virginia, and crossed the Potomac near the mouth of the South Branch, capturing the

---

forced back, and then the enemy advanced to this woods—Sumner's Corps, which was fresh, advancing on our left flank. My brigade then numbering about 1000 men for duty. with two or three hunred men of Jackson's own division, who had been rallied by Colonels Grigsby and Stafford, and when there was an interval of at least one half a mile between us and any other part of our line, held Sumner's Corps in check for some time, until Green's division of Mansfield's Corps penetrated into the interval in the woods between us and the rest of our line, when I was compelled to move by the flank and attack it. That division was driven out of the woods by my brigade, while Grigsby and Stafford skirmished with Sumner's advancing force, when we turned on it, and, with the aid of three brigades—to wit: Anderson's, Semmes', and Barksdale's—which had just arrived to our assistance, drove it from the woods in great confusion, and with heavy loss. So great was the disparity in the forces at this point that the wounded officers who were captured, were greatly mortified. and commenced making excuses by stating that the troops in their front were raw troops who stampeded and produced confusion in their ranks. McClellan, in his report, says that Sumner's Corps and Green's division encountered, in this woods, "overwhelming numbers behind breastworks," and he assigns the heavy losses and consequent demoralization in Sumner's Corps, as one of the reasons for not renewing the fight on the 18th We had no breastworks or anything like them in that woods on the 17th, and, on our part, it was a stand up fight there altogether. The slight breastworks subsequently seen by McClellan were made on the 18th when we were expecting a renewal of the battle.

    * For this act, I, alone, am responsible, as the officers engaged in it were simply executing my orders, and had no discretion left them. Notwithstanding the lapse of time which has occurred, and the result of the war, I am perfectly satisfied with my conduct on this occasion, and see no reason to regret it.

garrison at that place and partially destroying the railroad bridge. He then invested the post on the railroad at New Creek, but finding it too strongly fortified to take by assault, he moved to Moorefield in Hardy County, near which place he halted to rest and recruit his men and horses, as the command was now considered safe from pursuit. Averill, however, had been pursuing from Chambersburg with a body of cavalry, and Johnson's brigade was surprised in camp, before day, on the morning of the 7th of August, and routed by Averill's force. This resulted also in the rout of McCausland's brigade, and the loss of the artillery (4 pieces) and about 300 prisoners from the whole command. The balance of the command made its way to Mount Jackson in great disorder, and much weakened. This affair had a very damaging effect upon my cavalry for the rest of the campaign.*

RETREAT TO FISHER'S HILL, AND SUBSEQUENT OPERATIONS, UNTIL THE BATTLE OF WINCHESTER.

On the 9th., Imboden reported that a large force had been concentrated at Harper's Ferry, consisting of the 6th., 19th., and Crook's corps, under a new commander, and that it was moving towards Berryville, to our right. The new commander proved to be Major-General Sheridan, from Grant's army. On the 10th., we moved from Bunker Hill to the east of Winchester, to cover the roads from Charlestown and Berryville to that place ; and Ramseur's division was moved to Win-

---

* Grant says, in reference to this expedition under McCausland : " They were met and defeated by General Kelly; and, with diminished numbers, escaped into the mountains of West Virginia ; " and he makes no allusion whatever to Averill's affair. There was no defeat by Kelly, but there was one by Averill, as I have stated. This shows how loose Grant is as to his facts So far as we were concerned, the defeat by Averill was worse than it could have been by Kelly.

chester, to cover that place against a force reported to be advancing from the west; but, this report proving untrue, it was subsequently moved to the junction of the Millwood and Front Royal roads. On the morning of the 11th., it was discovered that the enemy was moving to our right, on the east of the Opequon, and my troops, which had been formed in line of battle covering Winchester, were moved to the right, towards Newtown, keeping between the enemy and the Valley Pike. Ramseur had a brisk skirmish with a body of the enemy's cavalry on the Millwood Road, and drove it back. Imboden's and Vaughan's brigades had a severe fight with another body of cavalry at the double toll-gate, at the intersection of the Front Royal road with the road from White Post to Newtown; and it was discovered that there had been a considerable accession to that arm from Grant's army. Just before night, Gordon had heavy skirmishing, near Newtown, with a large force of cavalry, which advanced on the road from the double toll-gate, and drove it off. We encamped near Newtown; and, on the morning of the 12th., moved to Hupp's Hill, between Strasburg and Cedar Creek. Finding that the enemy was advancing in much heavier force than I had yet encountered, I determined to take position at Fisher's Hill, above Strasburg, and await his attack there. Imboden, with his brigade, was sent to the Luray Valley, to watch that route; and, in the afternoon, we moved to Fisher's Hill. I had received information a few days before, from General Lee, that General Anderson had moved with Kershaw's division of infantry and Fitz Lee's division of cavalry to Culpepper C.H.; and I sent a dispatch to Anderson, informing him of the state of things, and requesting him to move to Front Royal, so as to guard the Luray Valley.

Sheridan's advance appeared on the banks of Cedar Creek, on the 12th., and there was some skirmishing with it. My troops were posted at Fisher's Hill, with the right resting on the North Fork of the Shenandoah, and the left extending towards Little North Mountain; and we awaited the advance of the enemy. General Anderson moved to Front Royal, in compliance with my request, and took position to prevent an advance of the enemy on that route. Shortly after I took position at Fisher's Hill, Major-General Lomax reported to me to relieve Ransom, in command of the cavalry, and Mc-Causland and Johnson joined us with the remnants of their brigades. Sheridan demonstrated at Hupp's Hill, within our view, for several days, and some severe skirmishing ensued.

Upon taking position at Fisher's Hill, I had established a signal-station on the end of Three Top Mountain, a branch of Massanutten Mountain, near Strasburg, which overlooked both camps and enabled me to communicate readily with General Anderson, in the Luray Valley. A small force from Sheridan's army ascended the mountain and drove off our signal-men, and possession was taken of the station by the enemy, who was in turn driven away; when several small but severe fights ensued over the station, possession of it being finally gained and held by a force of one hundred men under Captain Keller of Gordon's division.

On the morning of the 17th., it was discovered that the enemy was falling back, and I immediately moved forward in pursuit, requesting General Anderson, by signal, to cross the river at Front Royal, and move towards Winchester. Just before night, the enemy's cavalry and a body of infantry, reported to be a division, was encountered between Kernstown and Winchester, and driven through the latter place, after a sharp engagement, in which Wharton's division moved to the left and attacked the enemy's infantry, and drove it from a strong position on Bower's Hill, south of Winchester, while Ramseur engaged it in front, and Gordon advanced against the cavalry on the right.*

---

* When Hunter was relieved I had hoped that an end was put to his mode of warfare, but I had now to learn how the new commander proposed to carry on the war in behalf of "the best government the world ever saw," (so called). Sheridan had commenced burning barns, mills, and stacks of small grain and hay, and the whole country was smoking Among many others, the barn of a respectable farmer near Newtown, whose name was Chrisman, had been burned within a few steps of his house, and the latter saved with great difficulty, not-

On the 18th we took position to cover Winchester, and Gen. Anderson came up with Kershaw's division of infantry, Cutshaw's battalion of Artillery, and two brigades of cavalry under Fitz Lee. General Anderson ranked me, but he declined to take command, and offered to co-operate in any movement I might suggest. We had now discovered that Torbert's and Wilson's divisions of cavalry from Grant's army had joined Sheridan's force, and that the latter was very large.

On the 19th, my main force moved to Bunker Hill and Lomax's cavalry made reconnoissances to Martinsburg and Shepherdstown, while Anderson's whole force remained near Winchester.

On the 20th, our cavary had some skirmishing with the enemy's on the Opequon, and on the 21st, by concert, there was a general movement towards Harper's Ferry—my command moving through Smithfield towards Charlestown, and Anderson's on the direct road by Summit Point. A body of the enemy's cavalry was driven from the Opequon, and was pursued by part of our cavalry towards Summit Point. I encountered Sheridan's main force near Cameron's depot, about three

withstanding the fact that Mr. Chrisman had received from General Torbert, in command of the Federal cavalry, a written protection stating that for some weeks he had taken care of, and showed great kindness to, a badly-wounded Federal soldier. In passing through Middletown, I was informed that one of my soldiers had been tried and hung as a spy. The grave at the foot of the gallows was opened, and the body was recognized by his brother and the officers of his company as a private of the 54th North Carolina Regiment. This man had been found by the enemy in Middletown, in attendance on a Confederate soldier whose leg was amputated, and he had claimed to be a citizen, but a paper was found on his person showing that he had been formerly detailed as a nurse in the hospital. On this state of facts, he was hung as a spy. He was not employed in any such capacity, and he was so illiterate, not being able to read or write, that his appearance and evident want of intelligence precluded the idea of his being so employed. I would have retaliated at once by hanging a commissioned officer, but the enquiry which I made furnished some reason for believing that the man had remained behind, and endeavoured to pass for a citizen to avoid service in our army; and I did not therefore wish to risk the lives of my officers and men who were in the enemy's hands, by making his a case for retaliation. His execution by the enemy, however, was none the less wanton and barbarous.

miles from Charlestown, in a position which he commenced fortifying at once. Rodes' and Ramseur's divisions were advanced to the front, and very heavy skirmishing ensued and was continued until night, but I waited for General Anderson to arrive before making a general attack. He encountered Wilson's division of cavalry at Summit Point, and, after driving it off, went into camp at that place. At light next morning, it was discovered that the enemy had retired during the night, and his rear guard of cavalry was driven through Charlestown towards Hall-town, where Sheridan had taken a strong position under the protection of the heavy guns on Maryland Heights. I demonstrated on the enemy's front on the 22nd, 23rd, and 24th, and there was some skirmishing. General Anderson then consented to take my position in front of Charlestown and amuse the enemy with Kershaw's division of infantry, supported by McCausland's brigade of cavalry on the left and a regiment of Fitz Lee's cavalry on the right, while I moved with my infantry and artillery to Shepherdstown, and Fitz Lee with the rest of the cavalry to Williamsport, as if to cross into Maryland, in order to keep up the fear of an invasion of Maryland and Pennsylvania.

On the 25th Fitz Lee started by the way of Leetown and Martinsburg to Williamsport, and I moved through Leetown and crossed the railroad at Kearneysville to Shepherdstown. After Fitz Lee had passed on, I encountered a very large force of the enemy's cavalry between Leetown and Kearneysville, which was moving out with several days forage and rations for a raid in our rear. After a sharp engagement with small arms and artillery, this force was driven back through Shepherdstown, where we came very near surrounding and capturing a considerable portion of it, but it succeded in making its escape across the Potomac. Gordon's division, which was moved around to intercept the enemy, became heavily engaged, and cut off the retreat of part of his force by one road, but it made its way down the river to the ford by another and thus escaped. In this affair, a valuable officer, Colonel Monaghan of the 6th. Louisiana Regiment, was killed. Fitz Lee reached Williamsport, and had some skirmishing across the river at that place, and then moved to Shepherdstown.

On the 26th I moved to Leetown, and on the 27th I moved back to Bunker Hill; while Anderson, who had confronted Sheridan, during the two days of my absence, with but a division of infantry and a brigade and a regiment of cavalry, moved to Stephenson's Depot.

On the 28th, our cavalry, which had been left holding a line from Charlestown to Shepherdstown, was compelled to retire across the Opequon, after having had a brisk engagement with the enemy's cavalry at Smithfield. On the 29th, the enemy's cavalry crossed the Opequon near Smithfield, driving in our cavalry pickets, when I advanced to the front with a part of my infantry, and drove the enemy across the stream again, and, after a very sharp artillery duel, a portion of my command was crossed over and pursued the enemy through Smithfield towards Charlestown. We then retired, leaving a command of cavalry at Smithfield, but it was compelled to recross the Opequon, on the advance of a heavy force from the direction of Charlestown.

Quiet prevailed on the 30th, but on the 31st there were some demonstrations of cavalry by the enemy on the Opepuon, which were met by ours. On this day, (31st), Anderson moved to Winchester, and Rodes with his division went to Martinsburg on a reconnoissance, drove a force of the enemy's cavalry from that place, interrupted the preparations for repairing the railroad, and then returned.

There was quiet on the 1st, but, on the 2nd, I broke up my camp at Bunker Hill, and moved with three divisions of infantry and part of McCausland's cavalry under Col. Ferguson, across the country towards Summit Point, on a reconnoissance, while the trains under the protection of Rodes' division were moved to Stephenson's depot. After I had crossed the Opequon and was moving towards Summit Point, Averill's cavalry attacked and drove back in some confusion, first Vaughan's, and then Johnson's cavalry, which were on the Martinsburg road, and the Opequon, but Rodes returned towards

Bunker Hill and drove the enemy back in turn. This affair arrested my march and I recrossed the Opequon and moved to Stephenson's depot, where I established my camp.

On the 3rd, Rodes moved to Bunker Hill in support of Lomax's cavalry, and drove the enemy's cavalry from and beyond that place.

A letter had been received from General Lee, requesting that Kershaw's division should be returned to him, as he was very much in need of troops, and, after consultation with me, Gen. Anderson determined to recross the Blue Ridge with that division and Fitz Lee's cavalry. On the 3rd, he moved towards Berryville for the purpose of crossing the mountain at Ashby's Gap, and I was to have moved towards Charlestown next day, to occupy the enemy's attention during Anderson's movement. Sheridan, however, had started two divisions of cavalry through Berryville and White Post, on a raid to our rear, and his main force had moved towards Berryville. Anderson encountered Crook's corps at the latter place, and after a sharp engagement drove it back on the main body. Receiving information of this affair, I moved at daylight next morning, with three divisions, to Anderson's assistance, Gordon's division being left to cover Winchester. I found Kershaw's division extended out in a strong skirmish line confronting Sheridan's main force, which had taken position in rear of Berryville, across the road from Charlestown to that place, and was busily fortifying, while the cavalry force which had started on the raid was returning and passing between Berryville and the river to Sheridan's rear. As may be supposed, Anderson's position was one of great peril, if the enemy had possessed any enterprise, and it presented the appearance of the most extreme audacity for him thus to confront a force so vastly superior to his own, while, too, his trains were at the mercy of the enemy's cavalry, had the latter known it. Placing one of my divisions in line on Kershaw's left, I moved with the other two along the enemy's front towards his right, for the purpose of reconnoitring and attacking that flank, if a suitable opportunity offered. After moving in this way for two miles, I reached an elevated position from which the enemy's line was visible, and within artillery range of it. I at first thought that I had reached his right flank, and was about making arrangements to attack it, when casting my eye to my left, I discovered, as far as the eye could reach with the aid of field glasses, a line extending towards Summit Point. The position the enemy occupied was a strong one, and he was busily engaged fortifying it, having already made considerable progress. It was not until I had had this view that I realized the size of the enemy's force, and as I discovered that his line was too long for me to get around his flank, and the position was too strong to attack in front, I returned and informed General Anderson of the condition of things. After consultation with him, we thought it not advisable to attack the enemy in his entrenched lines, and we determined to move our forces back to the west side of the Opequon, and see if he would not move out of his works. The waggon trains were sent back early next morning (the 5th) towards Winchester, and, about an hour by sun, Kershaw's division, whose place had been taken by one of my divisions, moved towards the same point. About two o'clock in the afternoon my troops were withdrawn, and moved back to Stephenson's depot. This withdrawal was made while the skirmishers were in close proximity and firing at each other; yet there was no effort on the part of the enemy to molest us. Just as my front division (Rodes') reached Stephenson's depot, it met, and drove back, and pursued for some distance, Averill's cavalry, which was forcing, towards Winchester, that part of our cavalry which had been watching the Martinsburg road.

It was quiet on the 6th, but on the 7th the enemy's cavalry made demonstrations on the Martinsburg Road, and the Opequon at several points and was repulsed.

On the 8th it was quiet again, but on the 9th a detachment of the enemy's cavalry came to the Opequon below Brucetown, burned some mills, and retreated before a division of infantry sent out to meet it.

On the 10th, my infantry moved by Bunker Hill to Darkes

ville and encountered a considerable force of the enemy's cavalry, which was driven off, and then pursued by Lomax through Martinsburg across the Opequon. We then returned to Bunker Hill and the next day to Stephenson's depot, and there was quiet on the 12th.

On the 13th, a large force of the enemy's cavalry, reported to be supported by infantry, advanced on the road from Summit Point and drove in our pickets from the Opequon, when two divisions of infantry were advanced to the front, driving the enemy across the Opequon again. A very sharp artillery duel across the creek then took place, and some of my infantry crossed over, when the enemy retired.

On the 14th, General Anderson again started, with Kershaw's division and Cutshaw's battalion of artillery, to cross the Blue Ridge by the way of Front Royal, and was not molested. Fitz Lee's cavalry was left with me, and Ramseur's division was moved to Winchester to ocoupy Kershaw's position.

There was an affair between one of Kershaw's brigades and a division of the enemy's cavalry, while I was at Fisher's Hill and Anderson at Front Royal, in which some prisoners were lost; and two affairs in which the outposts from Kershaw's command were attacked and captured by the enemy's cavalry, one in front of Winchester and the other in front of Charlestown; which I have not undertaken to detail, as they occurred when General Anderson was controlling the operations of that division, but it is proper to refer to them here as part of the operations in the Valley.

On the 15th and 16th my troops remained in camp undisturbed.

The positions of the opposing forces were now as follows: Ramseur's division and Nelson's battalion of artillery were on the road from Berryville to Winchester, one mile from the latter place. Rodes', Gordon's, and Wharton's divisions, (the last two being under Breckenridge,) and Braxton's and King's battalions of artillery were at Stephenson's depot on the Winchester and Potomac railroad, which is six miles from Winchester. Lomax's cavalry picketed in my front on the Opequon, and on my left from that stream to North Mountain, while Fitz Lee's cavalry watched the right, having small pickets across to the Shenandoah. Four principal roads, from positions held by the enemy, centered at Stephenson's depot, to wit : the Martinsburg road, the road from Charlestown via Smithfield, the road from the same place via Summit Point, and the road from Berryville via Jordan's Springs. Sheridan's main force was near Berryville, at the entrenched position which has been mentioned, while Averill was at Martinsburg with a division of cavalry. Berryville is ten miles from Winchester, nearly east, and Martinsburg twenty two miles nearly north. The crossing of the Opequon on the Berryville road is four or five miles from Winchester. From Berryville there are two good roads to Front Royal, via Millwood and White Post, and from Millwood there is a macadamized road to Winchester, and also good roads via White Post to the Valley Pike at Newtown and Middletown, the last two roads running east of the Opequon. The whole country is very open, being a limestone country which is thickly settled and well cleared, and affords great facilities for the movement of troops and the operations of cavalry. From the enemy's fortifications on Maryland Heights, the country north and east of Winchester, and the main roads through it, are exposed to view.

The relative positions which we occupied rendered my communications to the rear very much exposed, but I could not avoid it without giving up the lower Valley. The object of my presence there was to keep up a threatening attitude towards Maryland and Pennsylvania, and prevent the use of the Baltimore and Ohio railroad, and the Chesapeake and Ohio canal, as well as to keep as large a force as possible from Grant's army to defend the Federal Capital. Had Sheridan, by a prompt movement, thrown his whole force on the line of my communications, I would have been compelled to attempt to cut my way through, as there was no escape for me to the right or left, and my force was too weak to cross the Potomac while he was in my rear. I knew my danger, but I could occupy no other position that would have enabled

me to accomplish the desired object. If I had moved up the
Valley at all, I could not have stopped short of New Market,
for between that place and the country in which I was there
was no forage for my horses ; and this would have enabled
the enemy to resume the use of the railroad and canal, and
return all the troops from Grant's army to him. Being compelled to occupy the position where I was, and being aware
of its danger as well as apprized of the fact that very great
odds were opposed to me, my only resource was to use my
forces so as to display them at different points with great
rapidity, and thereby keep up the impression that they were
much larger than they really were. The events of the last
month had satisfied me that the commander opposed to me
was without enterprise, and possessed an excessive caution
which amounted to timidity. If it was his policy to produce
the impression that his force was too weak to fight me, he did
not succeed, but if it was to convince me that he was not an
able or energetic commander, his strategy was a complete
success, and subsequent events have not changed my opinion.

My infantry force at this time consisted of the three divisions of the 2nd Corps of the Army of Northern Virginia, and
Wharton's division of Breckenridge's command. The 2nd
Corps numbered a little over 8000 muskets when it was
detached in pursuit of Hunter, and it had now been reduced
to about 7000 muskets, by long and rapid marches and the
various engagements and skirmishes in which it had participated. Wharton's division had been reduced to about 1700
muskets by the same causes. Making a small allowance for
details and those unfit for duty, I had about 8,500 muskets for
duty. When I returned from Maryland, my cavalry consisted of the remnants of five small brigades, to wit: Imboden's, McCausland's, Johnson's, Jackson's, and Vaughan's.
Vaughan's had now been ordered to South Western Virginia,
most of the men having left without permission. The surprise
and rout of McCausland's and Johnson's brigades by Averill
at Moorefield, had resulted in the loss of a considerable
number of horses and men, and such had been the loss in all

the brigades, in the various fights and skirmishes in which they had been engaged, that the whole of this cavalry, now under Lomax, numbered only about 1700 mounted men. Fitz Lee had brought with him two brigades, to wit: Wickham's, and Lomax's old brigade (now under Colonel Payne), numbering about 1200 mounted men. I had the three battalions of artillery which had been with me near Washington, and Fitz Lee had brought a few pieces of horse artillery. When I speak of divisions and brigades of my troops, it must be understood that they were mere skeletons of those organizations.

Since my return from Maryland, my supplies had been obtained principally from the lower Valley and the counties west of it, and the money which was obtained by contributions in Maryland was used for that purpose. Nearly the whole of our bread was obtained by threshing the wheat and then having it ground, by details from my command, and it sometimes happened that while my troops were fighting, the very flour which was to furnish them with bread for their next meal was being ground under the protection of their guns. Latterly our flour had been obtained from the upper Valley, but also by details sent for that purpose. The horses and mules, including the cavalry horses, were sustained almost entirely by grazing.

I have no means of stating with accuracy Sheridan's force, and can only form an estimate from such data as I have been able to procure. Citizens who had seen his force, stated that it was the largest which they had ever seen in the Valley on either side, and some estimated it as high as 60,000 or 70,000, but of course I made allowance for the usual exaggeration of inexperienced men. My estimate is from the following data: In Grant's letter to Hunter, dated at Monocacy, August 5th, 1864, and contained in the report of the former, is the following statement: " In detailing such a force, the brigade of cavalry now *en route* from Washington via Rockville, may be taken into account. There are now on their way to join you three other brigades of the best cavalry, numbering at least

5,000 men and horses." Sheridan relieved Hunter on the
6th, and Grant says in his report, " On the 7th of August, the
Middle Department and the Departments of West Virginia,
Washington, and the Susquehanna were constituted into the
Middle Military division, and Major General Sheridan was
assigned to the temporary command of the same.   Two
divisions of cavalry, commanded by Generals Torbert and
Wilson, were sent to Sheridan from the Army of the Potomac.
The first reached him at Harper's Ferry on the 11th of August."
Before this cavalry was sent to the Valley, there was already
a division there commanded by Averill, besides some detachments which belonged to the department of West Virginia.
A book containing the official reports of the chief surgeon of
the cavalry corps of Sheridan's army, which was subsequently
captured at Cedar Creek on the 19th of October, showed that
there were present for duty in that corps, during the first week
in September, over 11,000 men, and present for duty during
the week ending the 17th day of September, 10,100 men.
The extracts from Grant's report go to confirm this statement,
as, if three brigades numbered at least 5,000 men and horses,
the two divisions, when the whole of them arrived, with
Averill's cavalry, must have numbered over 10,000.   I think,
therefore, that I can safely estimate Sheridan's cavalry at the
battle of Winchester, on the 19th of September, at 10,000.
His infantry consisted of the 6th, 19th, and Crook's corps, the
latter being composed of the " Army of West Virginia," and
one division of the 8th corps.   The report of Secretary Stanton
shows that there was in the department of which the " Middle
Military division " was composed, the following " available
force present for duty May 1st, 1864," to wit :

" Department of Washington..........   42,124."
" Department of West Virginia.........   30,782."
" Department of the Susquehanna ......   2,970."
" Middle Department ....   5,627."

making an aggregate of 81,503 ; but, as the Federal Secretary
of War in the same report says, " In order to repair the losses
of the Army of the Potomac, the chief part of the force

designed to guard the Middle Department and the Department of Washington was called forward to the front," we may assume that 40,000 men were used for that purpose, which would leave 41,503, minus the losses in battle before Sheridan relieved Hunter, in the Middle Military division, exclusive of the 6th and 19th corps, and the cavalry from Grant's army. The infantry of the Army of the Potomac was composed of the 2nd, 5th, and 6th corps, on the 1st of May 1864, and Stanton says the " available force present for duty " in that army on that day, was 120,386 men. Allowing 30,000 for the artillery and cavalry of that army, which would be a very liberal allowance, and there would still be left 90,385 infantry ; and it is fair to assume that the 6th corps numbered one third of the infantry, that is, 30,000 men on the 1st of May 1864. If the losses of the Army of the Potomac had been such as to reduce the 6th corps to less than 10,000 men, notwithstanding the reinforcements and recruits received, the carnage in Grant's army must have been frightful indeed. The 19th corps was just from the Department of the Gulf and had not gone through a bloody campaign. A communication which was among the papers captured at Cedar Creek, in noticing some statement of a newspaper correspondent in regard to the conduct of that corps at Winchester, designated it as " a vile slander on 12,000 of the best soldiers in the Union army." In view of the foregoing data, without counting the troops in the Middle Department and the Departments of Washington and the Susquehanna, and making liberal allowances for losses in battle, and for troops detained on post and garrison duty in the Department of West Virginia, I think that I may assume that Sheridan had at least 35,000 infantry against me. The troops of the 6th corps and of the Department of West Virginia, alone, without counting the 19th corps, numbered on the 1st of May 1864, 60,782. If with the 19th corps, Sheridan did not have 35,000 infantry remaining from this force, what had become of the balance? Sheridan's artillery very greatly outnumbered mine, both in men and guns.

Having been informed that a force was at work on the railroad at Martinsburg, I moved on the afternoon of the 17th of September, with Rodes' and Gordon's division, and Braxton's artillery, to Bunker Hill, and, on the morning of the 18th, with Gordon's division and a part of the artillery to Martinsburg, preceded by a part of Lomax's cavalry. Averill's division of cavalry was driven from the town across the Opequon in the direction of Charlestown, and we then returned to Bunker Hill. Gordon was left at Bunker Hill, with orders to move to Stephenson's depot by sunrise next morning, and Rodes' division moved to the latter place that night, to which I also returned. At Martinsburg, where the enemy had a telegraph office, I learned that Grant was with Sheridan that day, and I expected an early move.

BATTLE OF WINCHESTER.

At light on the morning of the 19th, our cavalry pickets at the crossing of the Opequon on the Berryville road were driven in, and information having been sent me of that fact, I immediately ordered all the troops at Stephenson's depot to be in readiness to move, directions being given for Gordon, who had arrived from Bunker Hill, to move at once, but, by some mistake on the part of my staff officer, the latter order was not delivered to General Breckenridge or Gordon. I rode at once to Ramseur's position, and found his troops in line across the Berryville road skirmishing with the enemy. Before reaching this point, I had ascertained that Gordon was not moving, and sent back for him, and now discovering that the enemy's advance was a real one and in heavy force, I sent orders for Breckenridge and Rodes to move up as rapidly as possible. The position occupied by Ramseur, was about one mile and a half out from Winchester, on an elevated plateau between Abraham's Creek and Red Bud Run. Abraham's creek crosses the

Valley Pike one mile south of Winchester, and then crosses
the Front Royal road about the same distance south-east of the
town, and, running eastwardly, on the southern side of the
Berryville road, crosses that road a short distance before it
empties into the Opequon. Red Bud Run crosses the Martinsburg road about a mile and a half north of Winchester, and
runs eastwardly, on the northern side of the Berryville road, to
the Opequon. Ramseur was therefore in the obtuse angle
formed by the Martinsburg and Front Royal roads. In front
of and to the right of him, for some distance, the country was
open. Abraham's Creek runs through a deep valley, and beyond it, on the right, is high open ground, at the intersection
of the Front Royal and Millwood roads. To Ramseur's left,
the country sloped off to the Red Bud, and there were some
patches of woods which afforded cover for troops. To the
north of the Red Bud, the country is very open, affording facilities for the movement of any kind of troops. Towards the
Opequon, on the front, the Berryville road runs through a ravine
with hills and woods on each side, which enabled the enemy
to move his troops under cover, and mask them out of range of
artillery. Nelson's artillery was posted on Ramseur's line,
covering the approaches as far as practicable, and Lomax with
Jackson's cavalry and part of Johnson's was on the right,
watching the valley of Abraham's Creek and the Front Royal
road beyond, while Fitz Lee was on the left, across the Red
Bud, with his cavalry and a battery of horse artillery, and a
detachment of Johnson's cavalry watched the interval between
Ramseur's left and the Red Bud. These troops held the
enemy's main force in check until Gordon's and Rodes' divisions arrived from Stephenson's depot. Gordon's division
arrived first, a little after ten o'clock, A.M., and was placed
under cover in rear of a piece of woods behind the interval between Ramseur's line and the Red Bud, the detachment of
Johnson's cavalry having been removed to the right. Knowing
that it would not do for us to await the shock of the enemy's
attack, Gordon was directed to examine the ground on the left,
with a view to attacking a force of the enemy which had taken

position in a piece of wood in front of him, and while he was so engaged, Rodes arrived with three of his brigades, and was directed to form on Gordon's right in rear of another piece of woods. While this movement was being executed, we discovered very heavy columns of the enemy, which had been massed under cover between the Red Bud and the Berryville road, moving to attack Ramseur on his left flank, while another force pressed him in front. It was a moment of imminent and thrilling danger, as it was impossible for Ramseur's division, which numbered only about 1,700 muskets, to withstand the immense force advancing against it. The only chance for us was to hurl Rodes and Gordon upon the flank of the advancing columns, and they were ordered forward at once to the attack. They advanced in most gallant style through the woods into the open ground, and attacked with great vigour, while Nelson's artillery on the right, and Braxton's on the left, opened a destructive fire. But Evans' Brigade of Gordon's division, which was on the extreme left of our infantry, received a check from a column of the enemy, and was forced back through the woods from behind which it had advanced, the enemy following to the very rear of the woods, and to within musket range of seven pieces of Braxton's artillery which were without support. This caused a pause in our advance and the position was most critical, for it was apparent that unless this force was driven back the day was lost. Braxton's guns, in which now was our only hope, resolutely stood their ground, and, under the personal superintendence of Lieutenant Colonel Braxton and Colonel T. H. Carter, my then Chief of Artillery, opened with canister on the enemy. This fire was so rapid and well directed that the enemy staggered, halted, and commenced falling back, leaving a battle flag on the ground, whose bearer was cut down by a canister shot. Just then, Battle's brigade of Rodes' division, wnich had arrived and been formed in line for the purpose of advancing to the support of the rest of the division, moved forward and swept through the woods, driving the enemy before it, while Evans' brigade was rallied and brought back to the charge. Our advance, which had been suspended for a moment, was resumed, and the enemy's attacking columns were thrown into great confusion and driven from the field.   This attacking force of the enemy proved to be the 6th and 19th corps, and it was a grand sight to see this immense body hurled back in utter disorder before my two divisions, numbering a very little over 5,000 muskets.   Ramseur's division had received the shock of the enemy's attack, and been forced back a little, but soon recovered itself.   Lomax, on the right, had held the enemy's cavalry in check, and, with a part of his force, had made a gallant charge against a body of infantry, when Ramseur's line was being forced back, thus aiding the latter in recovering from the momentary disorder.   Fitz Lee on the left, from across the Red Bud, had poured a galling fire into the enemy's columns with his sharpshooters and horse artillery, while Nelson's and Braxton's battalions had performed wonders.   This affair occurred about 11, A.M., and a splendid victory had been gained.   The ground in front was strewn with the enemy's dead and wounded, and some prisoners had been taken.   But on our side, Major General Rodes had been killed, in the very moment of triumph, while conducting the attack of his division with great gallantry and skill, and this was a heavy blow to me.   Brigadier General Godwin of Ramseur's division had been killed, and Brigadier General York of Gordon's division had lost an arm.   Other brave men and officers had fallen, and we could illy bear the loss of any of them.   Had I then had a body of fresh troops to push our victory, the day would have been ours, but in this action, in the early part of the day, I had present only about 7,000 muskets, about 2,000 cavalry, and two battalions of artillery with about 30 guns; and they had all been engaged.   Wharton's division and King's artillery had not arrived, and Imboden's cavalry under Colonel Smith, and McCausland's under Colonel Ferguson, were watching the enemy's cavalry on the left, on the Martinsburg road and the Opequon.   The enemy had a fresh corps which had not been engaged, and there remained his heavy force of cavalry.   Our lines were now formed across from

Abraham's Creek to Red Bud and were very attenuated. The enemy was still to be seen in front in formidable force, and, away to our right, across Abraham's creek, at the junction of the Front Royal and Millwood roads, he had massed a division of cavalry with some artillery, overlapping us at least a mile, while the country was open between this force and the Valley Pike, and the Cedar Creek Pike back of the latter ; which roads furnished my only means of retreat in the event of disaster. My line did not reach the Front Royal road on the right, or the Martinsburg road on the left.

When the order was sent for the troops to move from Stephenson's depot, General Breckenridge had moved to the front, with Wharton's division and King's artillery, to meet a cavalry force which had driven our pickets from the Opequon on the Charlestown road, and that division had become heavily engaged with the enemy, and sustained and repulsed several determined charges of his cavalry, while its own flanks were in great danger from the enemy's main force on the right, and a column of his cavalry moving up the Martinsburg road on the left. After much difficulty and some hard fighting, Gen. Breckenridge succeeded in extricating his force, and moving up the Martinsburg road to join me, but he did not reach the field until about two o'clock in the afternoon.

In the meantime there had been heavy skirmishing along the line, and the reports from the front were that the enemy was massing for another attack, but it was impossible to tell where it would fall. As the danger from the enemy's cavalry on the right was very great and Lomax's force very weak, Wickham's brigade of Fitz Lee's cavalry had been sent from the left to Lomax's assistance. When Wharton's division arrived, Patton's brigade of that division was left to aid Fitz Lee in guarding the Martinsburg road, against the force of cavalry which was advancing on that road watched by Lomax's two small brigades ; and the rest of the division was formed in rear of Rodes' division in the centre, in order to be moved to any point that might be attacked. Late in the afternoon, two divisions of the enemy's cavalry drove in the small force which had been watching it on the Martinsburg road, and Crook's corps, which had not been engaged, advanced at the same time on that flank, on the north side of Red Bud, and, before this overwhelming force, Patton's brigade of infantry and Payne's brigade of cavalry under Fitz Lee were forced back. A considerable force of the enemy's cavalry then swept along the Martinsburg road to the very skirts of Winchester, thus getting in the rear of our left flank. Wharton's two other brigades were moved in double quick time to the left and rear, and, making a gallant charge on the enemy's cavalry, with the aid of King's artillery, and some of Braxton's guns which were turned to the rear, succeeded in driving it back. The division was then thrown into line by General Breckenridge, in rear of our left and at right angles with the Martinsburg road, and another charge of the enemy's cavalry was handsomely repulsed. But many of the men on our front line, hearing the fire in the rear, and thinking they were flanked and about to be cut off, commenced falling back, thus producing great confusion. At the same time, Crook advanced against our left, and Gordon threw Evans' brigade into line to meet him, but the disorder in the front line became so great, that, after an obstinate resistance, that brigade was compelled to retire also. The whole front line had now given way, but a large portion of the men were rallied and formed behind an indifferent line of breastworks, which had been made just outside of Winchester during the first year of the war, and, with the aid of the artillery which was brought back to this position, the progress of the enemy's infantry was arrested. Wharton's division maintained its organization on the left, and Ramseur fell back in good order on the right. Wickham's brigade of cavalry had been brought from the right, and was in position on Fort Hill just outside of Winchester on the west. Just after the advance of the enemy's infantry was checked by our artillery, it was reported to me that the enemy had got around our right flank, and as I knew this was perfectly practicable and was expecting such a movement from the cavalry on the Front Royal road, I gave the order to retire, but instantly discovering that the supposed force of the enemy was Ramseur's division, which had merely moved back to keep in line with the other troops, I gave the order for the latter to return to the works before they had moved twenty paces. This order was obeyed by Wharton's division, but not so well by the others. The enemy's cavalry force however was too large for us, and having the advantage of open ground, it again succeeded in getting around our left, producing great confusion, for which there was no remedy. Nothing was now left for us but to retire through Winchester, and Ramseur's division, which maintained its organization, was moved on the east of the town to the south side of it, and put in position forming the basis for a new line, while the other troops moved back through the town. Wickham's brigade, with some pieces of horse artillery on Fort Hill, covered this movement and checked the pursuit of the enemy's cavalry. When the new line was form-ed, the enemy's advance was checked until night-fall, and we then retired to Newtown without serious molestation. Lomax had held the enemy's cavalry on the Front Royal road in check, and a feeble attempt at pursuit was repulsed by Ram-seur near Kernstown.

As soon as our reverse began, orders had been sent for the removal of the trains, stores, and sick and wounded in the hospitals, to Fisher's Hill, over the Cedar Creek Pike and the Back Road. This was done with safety, and all the wounded, except such as were not in a condition to be moved, and those which had not been brought from the field, were carried to the rear.

This battle, beginning with the skirmishing in Ramseur's front, had lasted from daylight until dark, and, at the close of it, we had been forced back two miles, after having repulsed the enemy's first attack with great slaughter to him, and sub-sequently contested every inch of ground with unsurpassed obstinacy. We deserved the victory, and would have had it, but for the enemy's immense superiority in cavalry, which alone gave it to him.

Three pieces of King's artillery, from which the horses were shot, and which therefore could not be brought off, were lost, but the enemy claimed five, and, if he captured that number, two were lost by the cavalry and not reported to me. My loss in killed, wounded, and prisoners, was severe for the size of my force, but it was only a fraction of that claimed by the enemy. Owing to its obedience to orders in returning to the works, the heaviest loss of prisoners was in Wharton's division. Among the killed, were Major General Rodes and Brigadier General Godwin. Colonel G. W. Patton, commanding a brigade, was mortally wounded and fell into the hands of the enemy. Major General Fitz Lee was severely wounded, and Brigadier General York lost an arm. In Major General Rodes, I had to regret the loss, not only of a most accomplished, skilful, and gallant officer, upon whom I placed great reliance, but also of a personal friend, whose counsels had been of great service to me in the trying circumstances with which I had found myself surrounded. He fell at his post, doing a soldier's and patriot's duty to his country, and his memory will long be cherished by his comrades. General Godwin and Colonel Patton were both most gallant and efficient officers, and their loss was deeply felt, as was that of all the brave officers and men who fell in this battle. The enemy's loss in killed and wounded was very heavy, and some prisoners fell into our hands.

A skilful and energetic commander of the enemy's forces would have crushed Ramseur before any assistance could have reached him, and thus ensured the destruction of my whole force; and, later in the day, when the battle had turned against us, with the immense superiority in cavalry which Sheridan had, and the advantage of the open country, would have destroyed my whole force and captured everything I had. As it was, considering the immense disparity in numbers and equipment, the enemy had very little to boast of I had lost a few pieces of artillery and some very valuable officers and men, but the main part of my force, and all my trains had been saved, and the enemy's loss in killed and wounded was far greater than mine. When I look back to this battle, I can

but attribute my escape from utter annihilation to the inca-
pacity of my opponent.*

---

* The enemy has called this battle, "The Battle of the Opequon," but I know
no claim it has to that title, unless it be in the fact that, after his repulse in the
fore part of the day, some of his troops ran back across that stream. I have
always thought that instead of being promoted, Sheridan ought to have been
cashiered for this battle. He seems to be a sort of pet of Grant's, and I give
the following extracts from the report of the latter, to show the strange incon-
sistency of which he is guilty to magnify Sheridan's services. In his Monocacy
letter to Hunter, Grant says: "From Harper's Ferry if it is found that the
enemy has moved north of the Potomac in large force, push north following
him and attacking him wherever found ; follow him if driven south of the Potomac as long as it is safe to do so. If it is ascertained that the enemy has but a
small force north of the Potomac, then push south with the main force, detach-
ing under a competent commander, a sufficient force to look after the raiders
and drive them to their homes." And further on in the same letter, he says :
" Bear in mind the object is to drive the enemy south, and to do this, you want
to keep him always in sight. Be guided in your course by the course he takes."
When Sheridan relieved Hunter, this letter of instructions was ordered to be
turned over to him, and two divisions of cavalry subsequently joined him ; yet
Grant says in regard to Sheridan's operations : " His operations during the
month of August and the fore part of September, were both of an offensive and
defensive character, resulting in many severe skirmishes, principally by the
cavalry, in which we were generally successful, but no general engagement
took place. The two armies lay in such a position, the enemy on the west bank
of the Opequon Creek covering Winchester, and our forces in front of Berryville
—that either could bring on a battle at any time. Defeat to us would open to
the enemy the states of Maryland and Pennsylvania for long distances before
another army could be interposed to check him. Under these circumstances, I
hesitated about allowing the initiative to be taken. Finally the use of the
Baltimore and Ohio railroad and the Chesapeake and Ohio Canal, which were
both obstructed by the enemy, became so indispensablly necessary to us, and
the importance of relieving Pennsylvania and Maryland from continuously threatened invasion so great, that I determined the risk should be taken. But fearing
to telegraph the order for an attack without knowing more than I did of Gen.
Sheridan's feelings as to what would be the probable result, I left City Point
on the 15th of September to visit him at his head-quarters, to decide after con-
ference with him what should be done. I met him at Charlestown, and he
pointed out so directly how each army lay, *what he would do the moment he was
authorized,* and expressed such confidence of success that I saw there were but
two words of instruction necessary—go in." In the lteter to Hunter there is no
hesitation about the initiative, and yet, notwithstanding this letter was turned
over to Sheridan for his guidance, and two divisions of cavalry subsequently
sent to him, and the further fact that he had been operating both on the *offensive*
and defensive, during August and the fore part of September, the impression is
sought to be made, that his ardour was restrained by some sort of orders, of
which no mention is made in Grant's report. Really this is very curious, and

AFFAIR AT FISHER'S HILL.

At light on the morning of the 20th, my troops moved to Fisher's Hill without molestation from the enemy, and again took position at that point on the old line -- Wharton's division being on the right, then Gordon's, Ramseur's and Rodes', in the order in which they are mentioned. Fitz Lee's cavalry, now under Brigadier-General Wickham, was sent up the Luray Valley to a narrow pass at Millford, to try and hold that valley against the enemy's cavalry. General Ramseur was transferred to the command of Rodes' division, and Brigadier-General Pegram, who had reported for duty about the 1st of August, and been in command of his brigade since that time, was left in command of the division previously commanded by Ramseur. My infantry was not able to occupy the whole line at Fisher's Hill, notwithstanding it was extended out in an attenuated line, with considerable intervals. The greater part of Lomax's cavalry was therefore dismounted, and placed on Ramseur's left, near Little North Mountain, but the line could not then be fully occupied.

This was the only position in the whole Valley where a defensive line could be taken against an enemy moving up the Valley, and it had several weak points. To have retired beyond this point, would have rendered it necessary for me to fall back to some of the gaps of the Blue Ridge, at the upper part of the Valley, and I determined therefore to make a show

---

Grant's admission of his hesitation in allowing the initiative to be taken, and the statement that the Baltimore and Ohio Railroad and the Chesapeake and Ohio Canal were so obstructed, and the invasion of Pennsylvania and Maryland so constantly threatened, as to compel him to throw off that hesitation, convey a great compliment to the efficiency of my small force. The railroad is twenty-two miles from Winchester at the nearest point, and the canal over thirty and north of the Potomac, while Sheridan was much nearer to both. That Grant did find it necessary to say to Sheridan: "go in!" I can well believe, but that the latter was panting for the utterance of that classic phrase, I must be allowed to regard as apocryphal.

of a stand here, with the hope that the enemy would be deterred from attacking me in this position, as had been the case in August.

On the second day after our arrival at this place, General Breckenridge received orders from Richmond, by telegraph, to return to South Western Virginia, and I lost the benefit of his services. He had ably co-operated with me, and our personal relations had been of the most pleasant character.

In the afternoon of the 20th, Sheridan's forces appeared on the banks of Cedar Creek, about four miles from Fisher's Hill, and the 21st, and the greater part of the 22nd, were consumed by him in reconnoitring and gradually moving his forces to my front under cover of breast works. After some sharp skirmishing, he attained a strong position immediately in my front and fortified it, and I began to think he was satisfied with the advantage he had gained and would not probably press it further; but on the afternoon of the 22nd, I discovered that another attack was contemplated, and orders were given for my troops to retire, after dark, as I knew my force was not strong enough to resist a determined assault. Just before sunset, however, Crook's corps, which had moved to our left on the side of Little North Mountain, and under cover of the woods, forced back Lomax's dismounted cavalry, and advanced against Ramseur's left. Ramseur made an attempt to meet this movement by throwing his brigades successively into line to the left, and Wharton's division was sent for from the right but it did not arrive. Pegram's brigades were also thrown into line in the same manner as Ramseur's, but the movement produced some disorder in both divisions, and as soon as it was observed by the enemy, he advanced along his whole line, and the mischief could not be remedied. After a very brief contest, my whole force retired in considerable confusion, but the men and officers of the artillery behaved with great coolness, fighting to the very last, and I had to ride to some of the officers and order them to withdraw their guns, before they would move. In some cases, they had held out so long, and the roads leading from their positions into the Pike were so rugged, that eleven guns fell into the hands of the enemy. Vigorous pursuit was not made, and my force fell back through Woodstock to a place called the Narrow Passage, all the trains being carried off in safety.

Our loss in killed and wounded in this affair was slight, but some prisoners were taken by the enemy, the most of whom were captured while attempting to make their way across the North Fork to Massannutten Mountain, under the impression that the enemy had possession of the Valley Pike in our rear. I had the misfortune to lose my Adjutant General, Lieutenant Colonel A. S. Pendleton, a gallant and efficient young officer, who had served on General Jackson's staff during his Valley campaign, and subsequently to the time of the latter's death. Colonel Pendleton fell mortally wounded about dark, while posting a force across the Pike, a little in rear of Fisher's Hill, to check the enemy. He was acting with his accustomed gallantry, and his loss was deeply felt and regretted.*

RETREAT UP THE VALLEY, AND OPERATIONS UNTIL THE BATTLE OF CEDAR CREEK.

On the morning of the 23rd, I moved back to Mount Jackson, where I halted to enable the sick and wounded, and the hospital stores at that place to be carried off. In the afternoon Averill's division of cavalry came up in pursuit, and after

---

* In his account of the battle of Winchester, Grant says : "The enemy rallied and made a stand in a strong position at Fisher's Hill, where he was attacked and again defeated with heavy loss on the 20th." This makes Sheridan pursue and attack with great promptness and energy, if it were true, but it will be seen that the attack was not made until late on the afternoon of the 3rd day after the battle at Winchester, and that the movement on my left flank was again made by Crook. If Sheridan had not had subordinates of more ability and energy than himself, I should probably have had to write a different history of my Valley campaign.

some heavy skirmishing was driven back. I then moved to Rude's Hill between Mount Jackson and Newmarket.

On the morning of the 24th, a body of the enemy's cavalry crossed the North Fork below Mount Jackson, and attempted to get around my right flank, but was held in check The enemy's infantry soon appeared at Mount Jackson, and commenced moving around my left flank, on the opposite side of the river from that on which my left rested. As the country was entirely open, and Rude's Hill an elevated position, I could see the whole movement of the enemy, and as soon as it was fully developed, I commenced retiring in line of battle, and in that manner retired through New Market to a point at which the road to Port Republic leaves the Valley Pike, nine miles from Rude's Hill. This movement was made through an entirely open country, and at every mile or two a halt was made, and artillery opened on the enemy, who was pursuing, which compelled him to commence deploying into line, when the retreat would be resumed. In this retreat, under fire in line, which is so trying to a retiring force, and tests the best qualities of the soldier, the conduct of my troops was most admirable, and they preserved perfect order and their line intact, notwithstanding their diminished numbers, and the fact that the enemy was pursuing in full force, and, every now and then, dashing up with horse artillery under the support of cavalry, and opening on the retiring lines. At the last halt, which was at a place called "Tenth Legion," near where the Port Republic road leaves the Pike, and was a little before sunset, I determined to resist any further advance, so as to enable my trains to get on the Port Republic road ; and skirmishers were sent out and artillery opened on the advancing enemy, but, after some skirmishing, he went into camp in our view, and beyond the reach of our guns. At this point, a gallant officer of artillery, Captain Massie, was killed by a shell. As soon as it was dark, we retired five miles on the Port Republic road and bivouacked In the morning Lomax's cavalry had been posted to our left, on the Middle and Back roads from Mount Jackson to Harrisonburg, but it was forced back by a superior force of the enemy's cavalry, and retired to the latter place in considerable disorder. Wickham's brigade had been sent for from the Luray Valley to join me through the New-Market Gap but it arrived at that gap just as we were retiring through New-Market, and orders were sent for it to return to the Luray Valley, and join me at Port Republic. In the meantime, Payne's small brigade had been driven from Millford by two divisions of cavalry under Torbert, which had moved up the Luray Valley and subsequently joined Sheridan through the New-Market Gap. This cavalry had been detained by Wickham with his and Payne's brigades, at Millford, a sufficient time to enable us to pass New-Market in safety. If, however, it had moved up the Luray Valley by Conrad's store, we would have been in a critical condition.

On the morning of the 25th, we moved towards Port Republic, which is in the fork of the South Fork and South River, and where the road through Brown's Gap in the Blue Ridge crosses those rivers, in order to unite with Kershaw's division which had been ordered to join me from Culpepper C. H. We crossed the River below the junction, and took position between Port Republic and Brown's Gap. Fitz Lee's and Lomax's cavalry joined us here, and on the 26th, Kershaw's division with Cutshaw's battalion of artillery came up, after having crossed through Swift Run Gap, and encountered and repulsed, below Port Republic, a body of the enemy's cavalry. There was likewise heavy skirmishing on my front on the 26th with the enemy's cavalry, which made two efforts to advance towards Brown's Gap, both of which were repulsed after brisk fighting in which artillery was used

Having ascertained that the enemy's infantry had halted at Harrisonburg, on the morning of the 27th I moved out and drove a division of his cavalry from Port Republic, and then encamped in the fork of the rivers. I here learned that two divisions of cavalry under Torbert had been sent through Staunton to Waynesboro, and were engaged in destroying the railroad bridge at the latter place, and the tunnel through the Blue Ridge at Rockfish Gap, and, on the 28th, I moved for those points. In making this movement I had the whole of the enemy's infantry on my right, while one division of cavalry was in my rear and two in my front, and on the left was the Blue Ridge. I had therefore to move with great circumspection.—Wickham's brigade of cavalry was sent up South River, near the mountain, to get between the enemy and Rockfish Gap, while the infantry moved in two columns, one up South River with the trains guarded in front by Pegram's and Wharton's divisions, and in rear by Ramseur's division, and the other, composed of Kershaw's and Gordon's divisions with the artillery, on the right through Mount Meridian, Piedmont, and New Hope. McCausland's cavalry, under Colonel Ferguson, was left to blockade and hold Brown's Gap, while Lomax, with the rest of his cavalry and Payne's brigade, watched the right flank and rear. Wickham's brigade, having got between Rockfish Gap and Waynesboro, drove the enemy's working parties from the latter place, and took position on a ridge in front of it, when a sharp artillery fight ensued. Pegram's division, driving a small body of cavalry before it, arrived just at night and advanced upon the enemy, when he retired in great haste, taking the roads through Staunton and west of the Valley Pike, back to the main body. A company of reserves, composed of boys under 18 years of age, which had been employed on special duty at Staunton, had moved to Rockfish Gap, and another company of reserves from Charlottesville, with two pieces of artillery, had moved to the same point, and when the enemy advanced towards the tunnel and before he got in range of the guns, they were opened, and he retired to Waynesboro.

On the 29th and 30th, we rested at Waynesboro, and an engineer party was put to work repairing the bridge which had been but partially destroyed.

On the 1st of October, I moved my whole force across the country to Mount Sidney on the Valley Pike, and took position between that place and North River, the enemy's forces having been concentrated around Harrisonburg, and on the north bank of the river. In this position we remained until the 6th, awaiting the arrival of Rosser's brigade of cavalry which was on its way from General Lee's army. In the meantime there was some skirmishing with the enemy's cavalry on the North River, at the bridge near Mount Crawford and at Bridgewater above.*

On the 5th, Rosser's brigade arrived and was temporarily attached to Fitz Lee's division, of which Rosser was given the command, as Brigadier-General Wickham had resigned. The horses of Rosser's brigade had been so much reduced by previous hard service and the long march from Richmond, that the brigade did not exceed six hundred mounted men for duty when it joined me   Kershaw's division numbered 2700 muskets for duty, and he had brought with him Cutshaw's battalion of artillery.   These reinforcements about made up my losses at Winchester and Fisher's Hill, and I determined to attack the enemy in his position at Harrisonburg, and for that purpose made a reconnoissance on the 5th, but on the morning of the 6th, it was discovered that he had retired during the night down the Valley.†

---

* Grant says that, after the fight at Fisher's Hill, " Sheridan pursued him with great energy through Harrisonburg, Staunton, and the gaps of the Blue Ridge." With how much energy the pursuit was made, and how much truth there is in the statement that I was driven through "Harrisonburg, Staunton, and the gaps of the Blue Ridge," will be seen from the foregoing account. A portion of my cavalry passed through Harrisonburg, but none of my other troops, and none of them through Staunton, and I did not leave the Valley at all. Had Sheridan moved his infantry to Port Republic. I would have been compelled to retire through Brown's Gap to get provisions and forage, and it would have been impossible for me to return to the Valley until he evacuated the upper part of it.

† While Sheridan's forces were near Harrisonburg and mine were watching them, three of our cavalry scouts, in their uniforms and with arms, got around his lines near a little town called Dayton and encountered Lieutenant Meigs, a Federal Engineer officer, with two soldiers.   These parties came upon each other suddenly, and Lieutenant Meigs was ordered to surrender by one of our scouts, to which he replied by shooting and wounding the scout, who in his turn fired and killed the Lieutenant.   One of the men with Lieutenant Meigs was captured and the other escaped.   For this act Sheridan ordered the town of Dayton to be burned, but for some reason that order was countermanded, and another substituted for burning a large number of private houses in the neighborhood, which was executed, thus inflicting on non-combatants and women and children a most wanton and cruel punishment for a justifiable act of war.

When it was discovered that the enemy was retiring, I moved forward at once and arrived at New Market with my infantry on the 7th. Rosser pushed forward on the Back and Middle roads in pursuit of the enemy's cavalry, which was engaged in burning houses, mills, barns, and stacks of wheat and hay, and had several skirmishes with it, while Lomax also moved forward on the Valley Pike and the roads east of it. I halted at New Market with the infantry, but Rosser and Lomax moved down the Valley in pursuit, and skirmished successfully with the enemy's cavalry on the 8th; but on the 9th they encountered his whole cavalry force at Tom's Brook, in rear of Fisher's Hill, and both of their commands were driven back in considerable confusion, with a loss of some pieces of artillery,—nine were reported to me as the number lost, but Grant claims eleven. Rosser rallied his command on the Back Road, at Columbia furnace opposite Edinburg, but a part of the enemy's cavalry swept along the Pike to Mount Jackson, and then retired on the approach of a part of my infantry. On the 10th, Rosser established his line of pickets across the Valley from Columbia furnace to Edinburg, and on the 11th Lomax was sent to the Luray Valley to take position at Millford.

BATTLE OF CEDAR CREEK OR BELLE GROVE.

Having heard that Sheridan was preparing to send part of his troops to Grant, I moved down the Valley again on the 12th. On the morning of the 13th we reached Fisher's Hill, and I moved with part of my command to Hupp's Hill, between Strasburg and Cedar Creek, for the purpose of reconnoitring. The enemy was found posted on the North bank of Cedar Creek in strong force, and, while we were observing him, without displaying any of my force except a small body of cavalry, a division of his infantry was moved out to his left and stacked arms in an open field, when a battery of artillery was run out suddenly and opened on this division, scattering it in great confusion. The enemy then displayed a large force, and sent a division across the creek to capture the guns which had opened on him, but, when it had advanced near enough, Conner's brigade of Kershaw's division was sent forward to meet this division, and, after a sharp contest, drove it back in considerable confusion and with severe loss. Conner's brigade behaved very handsomely indeed, but unfortunately, after the enemy had been entirely repulsed, Brigadier-General Conner, a most accomplished and gallant officer, lost his leg by a shell from the opposite side of the creek. Some prisoners were taken from the enemy in this affair, and Colonel Wells, the division commander, fell into our hands mortally wounded. The object of the reconnoissance having been accomplished, I moved back to Fisher's Hill, and I subsequently learned that the 6th corps had started for Grant's army but was brought back after this affair.

I remained at Fisher's Hill until the 16th observing the enemy, with the hope that he would move back from his very strong position on the north of Cedar Creek, and that we would be able to get at him in a different position, but he did not give any indications of an intention to move, nor did he evince any purpose of attacking us, though the two positions were in sight of each other. In the meantime there was some skirmishing at Hupp's Hill, and some with the cavalry at Cedar Creek on the Back Road. On the 16th Rosser's scouts reported a brigade of the enemy's cavalry encamped on the Back Road, and detached from the rest of his force, and Rosser was permitted to go that night, with a brigade of infantry mounted behind the same number of cavalry, to attempt the surprise and capture of the camp. He succeeded in surrounding and surprising the camp, but it proved to be that of only a strong picket, the whole of which was captured—the brigade having moved its location.

At light on the morning of the 17th, the whole of my troops

were moved out in front of our lines, for the purpose of covering Rosser's return in case of difficulty, and, after he had
returned, General Gordon was sent with a brigade of his
division to Hupp's Hill, for the purpose of ascertaining by
close inspection whether the enemy's position was fortified,
and he returned with the information that it was. I was now
compelled to move back for want of provisions and forage, or
attack the enemy in his position with the hope of driving him
from it, and I determined to attack. As I was not strong
enough to attack the fortified position in front, I determined
to get around one of the enemy's flanks and attack him by
surprise if I could. After General Gordon's return from
Hupp's Hill, he and Captain Hotchkiss, my topographical
engineer, were sent to the signal station on the end of Massanutten Mountain, which had been re-established, for the
purpose of examining the enemy's position from that point,
and General Pegram was ordered to go as near as he could
to Cedar Creek on the enemy's right flank, and see whether
it was practicable to surprise him on that flank. Captain
Hotchkiss returned to my headquarters after dark, and reported
the result of his and General Gordon's examination, and he
gave me a sketch of the enemy's position and camps. He
informed me that the enemy's left flank, which rested near
Cedar Creek, a short distance above its mouth, was lightly
picketed, and that there was but a small cavalry picket on
the North Fork of the Shenandoah, below the mouth of the
creek, and he stated that, from information he had received,
he thought it was practicable to move a column of infantry
between the base of the mountain and the river, to a ford
below the mouth of the creek. He also informed me that the
main body of the enemy's cavalry was on his right flank on
the Back Road to Winchester. The sketch made by Captain
Hotchkiss, which proved to be correct, designated the roads
in the enemy's rear, and the house of a Mr. Cooley at a
favourable point for forming an attacking column, after it
crossed the river, in order to move against the enemy and
strike him on the Valley Pike in rear of his works. Upon

this information, I determined to attack the enemy by mov
ing over the ground designated by Captain Hotchkiss, if
it should prove practicable to move a column between the
base of the mountain and the river. Next morning, General
Gordon confirmed the report of Captain Hotchkiss, expressing
confidence that the attack could be successfully made on the
enemy's left and rear, and General Pegram reported that a
movement on the enemy's right flank would be attended with
great difficulty, as the banks of Cedar Creek on that flank
were high and precipitous and were well guarded. General
Gordon and Captain Hotchkiss were then sent to examine
and ascertain the practicability of the route at the base of the
mountain, and General Pegram, at his request, was permitted
to go to the signal station on the mountain to examine the
enemy's position himself from that point. Directions were
given, in the meantime, for everything to be in readiness to
move that night (the 18th), and the division commanders were
requested to be at my quarters at two o'clock in the afternoon,
to receive their final instructions.

The river makes a circuit to the left in front of the right of
the position at Fisher's Hill and around by Strasburg, leaving
a considerable body of land between it and the mountain, on
which are several farms. Whenever Fisher's Hill had been
occupied by us, this bend of the river had been occupied by a
portion of our cavalry, to prevent the enemy from turning the
right of the position, and it was now occupied by Colonel
Payne with his cavalry numbering about 300. In order to
make the contemplated movement, it was necessary to cross
the river into this bend, and then pass between the foot of the
mountain and the river below Strasburg, where the passage
was very narrow, and cross the river again below the mouth of
Cedar Creek. The enemy's camps and position were visible
from a signal station on Round Hill in rear of Fisher's Hill,
and had been examined by me from that point, but the distance was too great to see with distinctness. From the station
on the mountain, which immediately overlooked the enemy's
left, the view was very distinct, but I could not go to that

point myself, as the ascent was very rugged, and it required
several hours to go and come, and I could not leave my command for that time. I had therefore, necessarily, to rely on
the reports of my officers.

General Gordon and Captain Hotchkiss, on their return, reported the route between the mountain and river, which was
a blind path, to be practicable for infantry but not for artillery,
and a temporary bridge was constructed under Captain Hotchkiss's superintendence, at the first crossing of the river on our
right. The plan of attack on which I determined, was to send
the three divisions of the 2nd Corps, to wit: Gordon's, Ramseur's, and Pegram's, under General Gordon, over the route
which has been specified to the enemy's rear, to make the
attack at five o'clock in the morning, which would be a little
before day-break—to move myself, with Kershaw's and Wharton's divisions, and all the artillery, along the Pike through
Strasburg, and attack the enemy on the front and left flank
as soon as Gordon should become engaged, and for Rosser to
move with his own and Wickham's brigade, on the Back Road
across Cedar Creek, and attack the enemy's cavalry simultaneously with Gordon's attack, while Lomax should move by
Front Royal, cross the river, and come to the Valley Pike, so
as to strike the enemy wherever he might be, of which he was
to judge by the sound of the firing.

At two o'clock P.M., all the division commanders, except
Pegram, who had not returned from the mountain, came to
my head-quarters, and I gave them their instructions. Gordon
was directed to cross over into the bend of the river immediately after dark, and move to the foot of the mountain, where
he would rest his troops, and move from there in time to cross
the river again and get in position at Cooley's house in the
enemy's rear, so as to make the attack at the designated hour,
and he was instructed, in advancing to the attack, to move for
a house on the west side of the Valley Pike called the " Belle
Grove House," at which it was known that Sheridan's head-
quarters were located.—A guide who knew the country and
the roads, was ordered to be sent to General Gordon, and Col-

onel Payne was ordered to accompany him with his force of cavalry, and endeavour to capture Sheridan himself.—Rosser was ordered to move before day, in time to attack at five o'clock next morning, and to endeavour to surprise the enemy's cavalry in camp. Kershaw and Wharton were ordered to move, at one o'clock in the morning, towards Strasburg under my personal superintendence, and the artillery was ordered to concentrate where the Pike passed through the lines at Fisher's Hill, and, at the hour appointed for the attack, to move at a gallop to Hupp's Hill—the movement of the artillery being thus delayed for fear of attracting the attention of the enemy by the rumbling of the wheels over the macadamized road. Swords and canteens were directed to be left in camp, so as to make as little noise as possible. The division commanders were particularly admonished as to the necessity for promptness and energy in all their movements, and they were instructed to press the enemy with vigour after he was encountered, and to allow him no time to form, but to continue the pursuit until his forces should be completely routed. They were also admonished of the danger to be apprehended from a disposition to plunder the enemy's camps by their men, and they were enjoined to take every possible precaution against it.

Gordon moved at the appointed time, and, after he had started, General Pegram reported to me that he had discovered, from the signal station on the mountain, what he supposed to be an entrenchment thrown up across the road over which Gordon would have to advance after crossing the river the second time, and that the signal operators had informed him that it had been thrown up since Gordon and Hotchkiss made their examination ; and he suggested the propriety of attacking the enemy's left flank at the same time Gordon made his attack, as he would probably have more difficulty than had been anticipated. I adopted this suggestion, and determined to cross Kershaw's division over Cedar Creek, at Bowman's Mill, a little above its mouth, and strike the enemy's left flank simultaneously with the other attacks, of which purpose notice was sent to General Gordon by General Pegram.—At one o'clock on the morning of the 19th, Kershaw and Wharton moved, and I accompanied them. At Strasburg Kershaw moved to the right on the road to Bowman's Mill, and Wharton moved along the Pike to Hupp's Hill, with instructions not to display his forces but avoid the enemy's notice until the attack began, when he was to move forward, support the artillery when it came up, and send a force to get posession of the bridge on the Pike over the creek. I accompanied Kershaw's division, and we got in sight of the enemy's fires at half past three o'clock. The moon was now shining and we could see the camps. The division was halted under cover to await the arrival of the proper time, and I pointed out to Kershaw, and the commander of his leading brigade, the enemy's position and described the nature of the ground, and directed them how the attack was to be made and followed up. Kershaw was directed to cross his division over the creek as quietly as possible, and to form it into column of brigades as he did so, and advance in that manner against the enemy's left breastwork, extending to the right or left as might be necessary. At half past four he was ordered forward, and, a very short time after he started, the firing from Rosser on our left, and the picket firing at the ford at which Gordon was crossing were heard. Kershaw crossed the creek without molestation and formed his division as directed, and precisely at five o'clock his leading brigade, with little opposition, swept over the enemy's left work capturing seven guns, which were at once turned on the enemy. As soon as this attack was made, I rode as rapidly as possible to the position on Hupp's Hill to which Wharton and the artillery had been ordered. I found the artillery just arriving, and a very heavy fire of musketry was now heard in the enemy's rear from Gordon's column. Wharton had advanced his skirmishers to the creek capturing some prisoners, but the enemy still held the works on our left of the Pike, commanding that road and the bridge, and opened with his artillery on us. Our artillery was immediately brought into action and opened on the enemy, but he soon evacuated his works, and our men from the other columns rushed into them. Just then the sun rose, and Wharton's division and the artillery were immediately ordered forward. I rode in advance of them across the creek, and met General Gordon on the opposite hill. Kershaw's division had swept along the enemy's works on the right of the Pike, which were occupied by Crook's corps, and he and Gordon had united at the Pike, and their divisions had pushed across it in pursuit of the enemy. The rear division of Gordon's column (Pegram's) was crossing the river at the time Kershaw's attack was made, and General Gordon moved rapidly to Cooley's house, formed his troops and advanced against the enemy with his own division on the left, under Brigadier-General Evans, and Ramseur's on the right, with Pegram's in the rear supporting them. There had been a delay of an hour at the river before crossing it, either from a miscalculation of time in the dark, or because the cavalry which was to precede his column had not gotten up, and the delay thus caused, for which no blame is to be attached to General Gordon, enabled the enemy partially to form his lines after the alarm produced by Kershaw's attack, and Gordon's attack, which was after light, was therefore met with greater obstinacy by the enemy than it would otherwise have encountered, and the fighting had been severe. Gordon, however, pushed his attack with great energy, and the 19th and Crook's corps were in complete route, and their camps, with a number of pieces of artillery and a considerable quantity of small arms, abandoned. The 6th corps, which was on the enemy's right, and some distance from the point attacked, had had time to get under arms and take position so as to arrest our progress. General Gordon briefly informed me of the condition of things and stated that Pegram's division, which had not been previously engaged, had been ordered in. He then rode to take command of his division, and I rode forward on the Pike to ascertain the position of the enemy, in order to continue the attack. There was now a heavy fog, and that, with the smoke from the artillery and small arms, so obscured objects that the enemy's position could not be seen ; but I soon came to Generals Ramseur and Pegram, who informed me that Pegram's division had en-

countered a division of the 6th corps on the left of the Valley
Pike, and, after a sharp engagement, had driven it back on the
main body of that corps, which was in their front in a strong
position.   They further informed me that their divisions were
in line confronting the 6th corps, but that there was a vacancy
in the line on their right which ought to be filled.   I ordered
Wharton's division forward at once, and directed Generals
Ramseur and Pegram to put it where it was required.   In a
very short time, and while I was endeavouring to discover the
enemy's line through the obscurity, Wharton's division came
back in some confusion, and General Wharton informed me
that, in advancing to the position pointed out to him by
Generals Ramseur and Pegram, his division had been driven
back by the 6th corps, which, he said, was advancing.   He
pointed out the direction from which he said the enemy was
advancing, and some pieces of artillery, which had come up,
were brought into action.   The fog soon rose sufficiently for
us to see the enemy's position on a ridge to the west of
Middletown, and it was discovered to be a strong one.   After
driving back Wharton's division he had not advanced, but
opened on us with artillery, and orders were given for con-
centrating all our guns on him.   In the meantime, a force of
cavalry was advancing along the Pike, and through the fields
to the right of Middletown, thus placing our right and rear in
great danger, and Wharton was ordered to form his division
at once, and take position to hold the enemy's cavalry in
check.   Wofford's brigade of Kershaw's division, which had
become separated from the other brigades, was ordered up
for the same purpose.   Discovering that the 6th corps could
not be attacked with advantage on its left flank, because the
approach in that direction was through an open flat and across
a boggy stream with deep banks, I directed Captain Powell,
serving on General Gordon's staff, who rode up to me while
the artillery was being placed in position, to tell the General
to advance against the enemy's right flank, and attack it in
conjunction with Kershaw, while a heavy fire of artillery was
opened from our right; but as Captain Powell said he did not

know where General Gordon was, and expressed some doubt
about finding him, immediately after he started, I sent Lieutenant Page, of my own staff, with orders for both Generals
Gordon and Kershaw to make the attack. In a short time
Colonel Carter concentrated 18 or 20 guns on the enemy, and
he was soon in retreat. Ramseur and Pegram advanced at
once to the position from which the enemy was driven, and
just then his cavalry commenced pressing heavily on the right,
and Pegram's division was ordered to move to the north of
Middletown, and take position across the Pike against the cavalry. Lieutenant Page had returned and informed me that he
delivered my order to General Kershaw, but the latter informed
him that his division was not in a condition to make the attack, as it was very much scattered, and there was a cavalry
force threatening him in front. Lieutenant Page also stated
that he had seen Gordon's division in Kershaw's rear reform-
ing, and that it was also much scattered, and that he had not
delivered the order to General Gordon, because he saw that
neither his division nor Kershaw's was in a condition to execute it. As soon as Pegram moved, Kershaw was ordered
from the left to supply his place. I then rode to Middletown
to make provision against the enemy's cavalry, and discovered
a large body of it seriously threatening that flank, which was
very much exposed. Wharton's division and Wofford's brigade were put in position on Pegram's right, and several charges
of the enemy's cavalry were repulsed. I had no cavalry on
that flank except Payne's very small brigade, which had accompanied Gordon, and made some captures of prisoners and
waggons. Lomax had not arrived, but I received a message
from him, informing me that he had crossed the river after
some delay from a cavalry force guarding it, and I sent a message to him requiring him to move to Middletown as quick as
possible, but, as I subsequently ascertained, he did not receive
that message. Rosser had attacked the enemy promptly at
the appointed time, but he had not been able to surprise him,
as he was found on the alert on that flank, doubtless owing to
the attempt at a surprise on the night of the 16th. There was

now one division of cavalry threatening my right flank, and two were on the left, near the Back Road, held in check by Rosser. The force of the latter was too weak to make any impression on the enemy's cavalry, and all he could do was to watch it. As I passed across Cedar Creek after the enemy was driven from it, I had discovered a number of men in the enemy's camps plundering, and one of Wharton's battalions was ordered to clear the camps, and drive the men to their commands. It was reported to me, subsequently, that a great number were at the same work, and I sent all my staff officers who could be spared, to stop it if possible, and orders were sent to the division commanders to send for their men.

After he was driven from his second position, the enemy had taken a new position about two miles north of Middletown, and, as soon as I had regulated matters on the right so as to prevent his cavalry from getting in rear of that flank, I rode to the left, for the purpose of ordering an advance. I found Ramseur and Kershaw in line with Pegram, but Gordon had not come up. In a short time, however, I found him coming up from the rear, and I ordered him to take position on Kershaw's left, and advance for the purpose of driving the enemy from his new position—Kershaw and Ramseur being ordered to advance at the same time. As the enemy's cavalry on our left was very strong, and had the benefit of an open country to the rear of that flank, a repulse at this time would have been disastrous, and I therefore directed General Gordon, if he found the enemy's line too strong to attack with success, not to make the assault. The advance was made for some distance, when Gordon's skirmishers came back reporting a line of battle in front behind breast works, and General Gordon did not make the attack. It was now apparent that it would not do to press my troops further. They had been up all night and were much jaded. In passing over rough ground to attack the enemy in the early morning, their own ranks had been much disordered, and the men scattered, and it had required time to reform them. Their ranks, moreover, were much thinned by the absence of the men engaged in plundering the enemy's camps. The delay which had unavoidably occurred, had enabled the enemy to rally a portion of his routed troops, and his immense force of cavalry, which remained intact, was threatening both of our flanks in an open country, which of itself rendered an advance extremely hazardous. I determined, therefore, to try and hold what had been gained, and orders were given for carrying off the captured and abandoned artillery, small arms, and waggons. A number of bold attempts were made during the subsequent part of the day, by the enemy's cavalry, to break our line on the right, but they were invariably repulsed. Late in the afternoon, the enemy's infantry advanced against Ramseur's, Kershaw's and Gordon's lines, and the attack on Ramseur's and Kershaw's fronts was handsomely repulsed in my view, and I hoped that the day was finally ours, but a portion of the enemy had penetrated an interval which was between Evans' brigade, on the extreme left, and the rest of the line, when that brigade gave way, and Gordon's other brigades soon followed. General Gordon made every possible effort to rally his men, and lead them back against the enemy, but without avail. The information of this affair, with exaggerations, passed rapidly along Kershaw's and Ramseur's lines, and their men, under the apprehension of being flanked, commenced falling back in disorder, though no enemy was pressing them, and this gave me the first intimation of Gordon's condition. At the same time the enemy's cavalry, observing the disorder in our ranks, made another charge on our right, but was again repulsed. Every effort was made to stop and rally Kershaw's and Ramseur's men, but the mass of them resisted all appeals, and continued to go to the rear without waiting for any effort to retrieve the partial disorder. Ramseur, however, succeeded in retaining with him two or three hundred men of his division, and Major Goggin of Kershaw's staff, who was in command of Conner's brigade, about the same number from that brigade; and these men, with six pieces of artillery of Cutshaw's battalion held the enemy's whole force on our left in check for one hour and a half, until Ramseur was shot down mortally wounded, and the ammunition of those pieces of artillery was exhausted. While the latter were being replaced by other guns, the force that had remained with Ramseur and Goggin gave way also. Pegram's and Wharton's divisions, and Wofford's brigade had remained steadfast on the right, and resisted all efforts of the enemy's cavalry, but no portion of this force could be moved to the left without leaving the Pike open to the cavalry, which would have destroyed all hope at once. Every effort to rally the men in the rear having failed, I had now nothing left for me but to order these troops to retire also. When they commenced to move, the disorder soon extended to them, but General Pegram succeeded in bringing back a portion of his command across Cedar Creek in an organized condition, holding the enemy in check, but this small force soon dissolved. A part of Evans' brigade had been rallied in the rear, and held a ford above the bridge for a short time, but it followed the example of the rest. I tried to rally the men immediately after crossing Cedar Creek, and at Hupp's Hill, but without success. Could 500 men have been rallied, at either of these places, who would have stood by me, I am satisfied that all my artillery and waggons and the greater part of the captured artillery could have been saved, as the enemy's pursuit was very feeble. As it was, a bridge broke down on a very narrow part of the road between Strasburg and Fisher's Hill, just above Strasburg, where there was no other passway, thereby blocking up all the artillery, ordnance and medical waggons, and ambulances which had not passed that point ; and, as there was no force to defend them, they were lost, a very small body of the enemy's cavalry capturing them.

The greater part of the infantry was halted at Fisher's Hill, and Rosser, whose command had retired in good order on the Back Road, was ordered to that point with his cavalry. The infantry moved back towards New Market at three o'clock next morning, and Rosser was left at Fisher's Hill to cover the retreat of the troops, and hold that position until they were beyond pursuit. He remained at Fisher's Hill until after ten o'clock on the 20th, and the enemy did not advance to that place while he was there.   He then fell back without molestation to his former position, and established his line on Stony Creek, across from Columbia Furnace to Edinburg, seven miles below Mount Jackson.   My other troops were halted at New Market, about seven miles from Mount Jackson, and there was an entirely open conntry between the two places, they being very nearly in sight of each other.*

Lomax had moved, on the day of the battle, on the Front Royal road towards Winchester, under the impression that the enemy was being forced back towards that place, and he did not reach me.   When he ascertained the reverse which had taken place in the latter part of the day, he retired up the Luray Valley to his former position at Millford, without molestation.

My loss in the battle of Cedar Creek was twenty-three pieces of artillery, some ordnance and medical waggons and ambulances, which had been carried to the front for the use of the troops on the field, about 1860 in killed and wounded, and something over 1,000 prisoners.   Major General Ramseur fell into the hands of the enemy mortally wounded, and in him, not only my command, but the country sustained a heavy loss. He was a most gallant and energetic officer whom no disaster appalled, but his courage and energy seemed to gain new

---

* Grant says in his account of the battle of Cedar Creek : " The enemy was defeated with great slaughter, and the loss of the most of his artillery and trains, and the trophies he had captured in the morning. The wreck of his army escaped during the night, and fled in the direction of Staunton and Lynchburg. Pursuit was made to Mount Jackson." Stanton, who seems to think it his duty to improve on all Grant's statements, says : " The routed forces of the enemy were pursued to Mount Jackson, where he arrived without an organized regiment of his army. All of his artillery, and thousands of prisoners fell into Sheridan's hands. These successes closed military operations in the Shenandoah Valley, and *a rebel force appeared there no more during the war.*" The recklessnes of these statements, of both Grant and Stanton, will appear trom the above narrative, as well as from my subsequent operations in the Shenandoah Valley. Would it be believed that this wreck of my army, which fled in such wild dismay before its pursuers, carried from the battle field 1500 prisoners, who were sent to Richmond—subsequently confronted Sheridan's whole force north of Cedar Creek, for two days, without his attacking it, and sent out expeditions which captured two important posts, with over 1000 prisoners and several pieces of artillery, in the limits of Sheridan's command ? Yet such was the case.

strength in the midst of confusion and disorder. He fell at his post fighting like a lion at bay, and his native state has reason to be proud of his memory. Brigadier General Battle was wounded at the beginning of the fight, and other valuable officers were lost. Fifteen hundred prisoners were captured from the enemy and brought off, and his loss in killed and wounded in this action was very heavy.

This was the case of a glorious victory given up by my own troops after they had won it, and it is to be accounted for, on the ground of the partial demoralization caused by the plunder of the enemy's camps, and from the fact that the men undertook to judge for themselves when it was proper to retire. Had they but waited, the mischief on the left would have been remedied. I have never been able to satisfy myself that the enemy's attack, in the afternoon, was not a demonstration to cover his retreat during the night. It certainly was not a vigorous one, as is shown by the fact that the very small force with Ramseur and Goggin held him in check so long; and the loss in killed and wounded in the division which first gave way, was not heavy, and was the least in numbers of all but one, though it was the third in strength, and its relative loss was the least of all the divisions. I read a sharp lecture to my troops, in an address published to them a few days after the battle, but I have never attributed the result to a want of courage on their part, for I had seen them perform too many prodigies of valour to doubt that. There was an individuality about the Confederate soldier, which caused him to act often in battle according to his own opinions, and thereby impair his own efficiency; and the tempting bait offered by the rich plunder of the camps of the enemy's well fed, and well clothed troops, was frequently too great for our destitute soldiers, and caused them to pause in the career of victory.

Had my cavalry been sufficient to contend with that of the enemy, the rout in the morning would have been complete; as it was, I had only about 1200 cavalry on the field under Rosser, and Lomax's force, which numbered less than 1700, did not get up. My infantry and artillery was about the same

strength as at Winchester. The reports of the Ordnance officers showed in the hands my troops about 8,800 muskets, in
round numbers as follows : in Kershaw's division 2,700, Ramseur's 2,100, Gordon's 1,700, Pegram's 1,200, and Wharton's
1,100. Making a moderate allowance for the men left to guard
the camps and the signal station on the mountain, as well as
for a few sick and wounded, I went into this battle with about
8,500 muskets and a little over forty pieces of artillery.

The book containing the reports of the Chief Surgeon of
Sheridan's cavalry corps, which has been mentioned as captured at this battle, showed that Sheridan's cavalry numbered
about 8,700 men for duty a few days previous, and from information which I had received of reinforcements sent him, in
the way of recruits and returned convalescents, I am satisfied
that his infantry force was fully as large as at Winchester.
Sheridan was absent in the morning at the beginning of the
fight, and had returned in the afternoon before the change in
the fortunes of the day. Nevertheless, I saw no reason to
change the estimate I had formed of him *

It may be asked, why with my small force I made the
attack ? I can only say we had been fighting large odds
during the whole war, and I knew there was no chance of
lessening them. It was of the utmost consequence that Sheridan should be prevented from sending troops to Grant, and
General Lee, in a letter received a day or two before, had
expressed an earnest desire that a victory should be gained
in the Valley if possible, and it could not be gained without
fighting for it. I did hope to gain one by surprising the enemy
in his camp, and then thought and still think I would have had
it, if my directions had been strictly complied with, and my
troops had awaited my orders to retire.†

---

* The retreat of the main body of his army had been arrested, and a new line
formed behind breastworks of rails, before Sheridan arrived on the field ; and he
still had immense odds against me when he made the attack in the afternoon.

† A silly story was circulated and even published in the papers, that this battle was planned and conducted by one of my subordinates up to a certain point,
when my arrival on the field stopped the pursuit and arrested the victory. No

CLOSE OF THE VALLEY CAMPAIGN.

After the return from Cedar Creek, the main body of my troops remained in their camp for the rest of the month without disturbance, but on the 26th of October the enemy's cavalry attacked Lomax at Millford and, after sharp fighting, was repulsed. Having heard that Sheridan was preparing to send troops to Grant, and that the Manassas Gap railroad was being repaired, I moved down the Valley again on the 10th of November. I had received no reinforcements except about 350 cavalry under General Cosby from Breckenridge's department in South Western Virginia, some returned convalescents, and several hundred conscripts who had been on details which had been revoked. On the 11th, on our approach to Cedar Creek, it was found that the enemy had fallen back towards Winchester, after having fortified and occupied a position on Hupp's Hill subsequently to the battle of Cedar Creek. Col. Payne drove a small body of cavalry through Middletown to Newtown, and I followed him and took position south of the latter place and in view of it. Sheridan's main force was found posted north of Newtown in a position which he was engaged in fortifying. I remained in front of him during the 11th and 12th, Rosser being on my left flank on the Back

---

officer or soldier on that day received an order from me to halt, unless he was going to the rear. My orders were to press the enemy from the beginning and give him no time to form, and when I found that my troops had halted, I endeavoured to advance again, but I discovered it would not do to press them further. Those who have known me from my youth, as well as those who came in contact with me during the war, know that I was not likely to permit any other to plan a battle for me, or assume my duties in any particular. Yet I was always willing to receive and adopt valuable suggestions from any of my officers.

There was another false report, as to my personal habits during the Valley Campaign, which obtained some circulation and credence, but which I would not notice, except for the fact that it was referred to on the floor of the Confederate Senate by two members of that body. The utter falsehood of this report was well known to all my staff and General officers, as well as to all others who associated with me.

Road, and Lomax on my right between the Valley Pike and the Front Royal road, with one brigade (McCausland's) at Cedarville on the latter road. Rosser had some skirmishing with the enemy's cavalry on the 11th, and on the 12th two divisions advanced against him, and after a heavy fight the enemy was repulsed and some prisoners captured. Colonel Payne, who was operating immediately in my front, likewise had a sharp engagement with a portion of the enemy's cavalry and defeated it. When Rosser was heavily engaged, Lomax was ordered to his assistance with a part of his command, and, during his absence, late in the afternoon, Powell's division of the enemy's cavalry attacked McCausland at Cedarville, and, after a severe fight, drove him back across the river with the loss of two pieces of artillery. At the time of this affair, a blustering wind was blowing and the firing could not be heard ; and nothing was known of McCauslands misfortune until after we commenced retiring that night. In these cavalry fights, three valuable officers were killed, namely : Lt.-Col. Marshall of Rosser's brigade, Col. Radford of McCausland's brigade, and Capt. Harvie of McCausland's staff.

Discovering that the enemy continued to fortify his position, and showed no disposition to come out of his lines with his infantry, and not being willing to attack him in his entrenchments, after the reverses I had met with, I determined to retire, as we were beyond the reach of supplies. After dark on the 12th, we moved to Fisher's Hill, and next day returned in the direction of New-Market, where we arrived on the 14th, no effort at pursuit being made. I discovered by this movement that no troops had been sent to Grant, and that the project of repairing the Manassas Gap rail-road had been abandoned.*

Shortly after our return to New-Market, Kershaw's division was returned to General Lee, and Cosby's cavalry to Breck-

---

* From Grant's account of the battle of Cedar Creek, it would be supposed that the 6th corps was returned to the army of the Potomac immediately after that battle, but the truth is that no troops were sent from Sheridan's army until in December, when the cold weather had put an end to all operations in the field by infantry.

enridge. On the 22nd of November two divisions of the enemy's cavalry advanced to Mount Jackson, after having driven in our cavalry pickets. A part of it crossed over the river into Meem's bottom at the foot of Rude's Hill, but was driven back by a portion of my infantry, and the whole retreated, being pursued by Wickham's brigade, under Colonel Munford, to Woodstock.

On the 27th, Rosser crossed Great North Mountain into Hardy County, with his own and Payne's brigade, and, about the 29th, surprised and captured the fortified post at New Creek, on the Baltimore and Ohio rail-road. At this place, two regiments of cavalry with their arms and colours were captured, and eight pieces of artillery and a very large amount of ordnance, quarter master, and commissary stores fell into our hands. The prisoners, numbering 800, four pieces of artillery, and some waggons and horses, were brought off, the other guns, which were heavy siege pieces, being spiked, and their carriages and a greater part of the stores destroyed. Rosser also brought off several hundred cattle and a large number of sheep from Hampshire and Hardy counties.

This expedition closed the material operations of the campaign of 1864 in the Shenandoah Valley, and, at that time, the enemy held precisely the same portion of that valley, which he held before the opening of the campaign in the spring, and no more, and the headquarters of his troops were at the same place, to wit: Winchester. There was this difference however: at the beginning of the campaign, he held it with comparatively a small force, and at the close, he was compelled to employ three corps of infantry and one of cavalry, for that purpose, and to guard the approaches to Washington, Maryland, and Pennsylvania. When I was detached from General Lee's army, Hunter was advancing on Lynchburg, 170 miles south of Winchester, with a very considerable force, and threatening all of General Lee's communications with a very serious danger. By a rapid movement, my force had been thrown to Lynchburg, just in time to arrest Hunter's march into that place, and he had been driven back and forced to escape into the mountains of Western Virginia, with a loss of ten pieces of artillery, and subsequent terrible suffering to his troops.   Maryland and Pennyslvania had been invaded, Washington threatened and thrown into a state of frantic alarm, and Grant had been compelled to detach two corps of infantry and two divisions of cavalry from his army.   Five or six thousand prisoners had been captured from the enemy and sent to Richmond, and, according to a published statement by Sheridan, his army had lost 13,831, in killed and wounded, after he took command of it.   Heavy losses had been inflicted on that army by my command, before Sheridan went to the Valley, and the whole loss could not have been far from double my entire force.   The enemy moreover had been deprived of the use of the Baltimore and Ohio rail-road, and the Chesapeake and Ohio canal, for three months.   It is true that I had lost many valuable officers and men, and about 60 pieces of artillery, counting those lost by Ramseur and McCausland, and not deducting the 19 pieces captured from the enemy ; but I think I may safely state that the fall of Lynchburg with its foundries and factories, and the consequent destruction of General Lee's communications, would have rendered necessary the evacuation of Richmond, and that, therefore, the fall of the latter place had been prevented ; and, by my subsequent operations, Grant's operations against General Lee's army had been materially impeded, and for some time substantially suspended.

My loss in killed, wounded, and prisoners, at Winchester and Fisher's Hill, had been less than 4,000, and, at Cedar Creek, about 3,000, but the enemy has attempted to magnify it to a much larger figure, claiming as prisoners several thousand more than my entire loss.   How he makes out his estimate is not for me to explain.   He was never scrupulous as to the kinds of persons of whom he made prisoners, and the statements of the Federal officers were not always confined to the truth, as the world has probably learned.   I know that a number of prisoners fell into the enemy's hands, who did not belong to my command : such as cavalry men on details to get fresh horses, soldiers on leave of absence, conscripts on special details, citizens not in the service, men employed in getting supplies for the departments, and stragglers and deserters from other commands.

My army during the entire campaign had been self sustaining, so far as provisions and forage were concerned, and a considerable number of beef cattle had been sent to General Lee's army ; and when the difficulties under which I laboured are considered, I think I may confidently assert that I had done as well as it was possible for me to do.*

---

* Some attempts have been made to compare my campaign in the Valley with that of General Jackson in the same district, in order to cast censure on me, but such comparison is not necessary for the vindication of the fame of that great leader, and it is most unjust to me, as the circumstances under which we operated were so entirely dissimilar. It was my fortune to serve under General Jackson, after his Valley campaign until his death, and I have the satisfaction of knowing that I enjoyed his confidence, which was signally shown in his last official act towards me ; and no one admires his character and reveres his memory more than I do. It is not therefore with any view to detract from his merits, that I mention the following facts, but to show how improper it is to compare our campaigns, with a view of contrasting their merits. 1st. General Jackson did not have the odds opposed to him which I had, and his troops were composed entirely of the very best material which entered into the composition of our armies, that is, the men who came out voluntarily in the beginning of the war ; while my command, though comprising all the principal organizations which were with him, did not contain 1,500 of the men who had participated in the first Valley campaign, and there was a like falling off in the other organizations with me, which had not been with General Jackson in that campaign. This was owing to the losses in killed and disabled, and prisoners who were not exchanged. Besides the old soldiers whose numbers were so reduced, my command was composed of recruits and conscripts. 2nd. General Jackson's cavalry was not outnumbered by the enemy's, and it was far superior in efficiency—Ashby being a host in himself; while my cavalry was more than trebled in numbers, and far excelled in arms, equipments, and horses, by that of the enemy. 3rd. The Valley, at the time of his campaign, was teeming with provisions and forage from one end to the other ; while my command had very great difficulty in obtaining provisions for the men, and had to rely almost entirely on the grass in the open fields for forage. 4th. When General Jackson was pressed and had to retire, as well when he fell back before Banks in the spring of 1862, as, later, when he retired before Fremont to prevent Shields from getting in his rear, the condition of the water courses was such as to enable him to stop the advance of one column, by burning the bridges, and then fall upon and defeat another column ; and, when hard pressed, place his troops in a position of security, until a favorable opportunity offered for attacking the enemy ; while all the water

Shortly after Rosser's return from the New Creek expedition, Colonel Munford was sent with Wickham's brigade to the counties of Hardy and Pendleton, to procure forage for his horses, and, cold weather having now set in so as to prevent material operations in the field, the three divisions of the 2nd Corps were sent, in succession, to general Lee,—Wharton's division, the cavalry, and most of the artillery being retained with me.

On the 16th of December, I broke up the camp at New-Market, and moved back towards Staunton, for the purpose of establishing my troops on or near the Central rail-road—Lomax's cavalry, except one brigade left to watch the Luray Valley, having previously moved across the Blue Ridge, so as to be able to procure forage. Cavalry pickets were left in front of New-Market, and telegraphic communications kept up with that place, from which there was communication with the lower Valley, by means of signal stations on the northern end of Massanutten Mountain, and at Ashby's Gap in the Blue Ridge, which overlooked the enemy's camps and the surrounding country.

The troops had barely arrived at their new camps, when information was received that the enemy's cavalry was in motion. On the 19th, Custer's division moved from Winchester towards Staunton, and, at the same time, two other divisions of cavalry, under Torbert or Merrit, moved across by Front Royal and Chester Gap towards Gordonsville. This information having been sent me by signal and telegraph, Wharton's division was moved, on the 20th, through a hailstorm, towards Harrisonburg, and Rosser ordered to the front with all the cavalry he could collect. Custer's division reached Lacy's Spring, nine miles north of Harrisonburg, on the evening of the 20th, and, next morning before day, Rosser,

---

courses were low and fordable, and the whole country was open in my front, on my flanks, and in my rear, during my entire campaign. These facts do not detract from the merits of General Jackson's campaign in the slightest degree, and far be it from me to attempt to obscure his well earned and richly deserved fame. They only show that I ought not to be condemned for not doing what he did.

with about 600 men of his own and Payne's brigades, attacked it in camp, and drove it back down the Valley in some confusion. Lomax had been advised of the movement towards Gordonsville, and, as soon as Custer was disposed of, Wharton's division was moved back, and on the 23rd a portion of it was run on the railroad to Charlottesville—Munford, who had now returned from across the great North Mountain, being ordered to the same place. On my arrival at Charlottesville on the 23rd, I found that the enemy's two divisions of cavalry, which had crossed the Blue Ridge, had been held in check near Gordonsville by Lomax, until the arrival of a brigade of infantry from Richmond, when they retired precipitately. I returned to the Valley and established my head quarters at Staunton—Wharton's division and the artillery being encamped east of that place, and Rosser's cavalay west of it; and thus closed the operations of 1864 with me.*

---

* At the close of the year 1864, Grant's plans for the campaign in Virginia had been baffled, and he had merely attained a position on James River, which he might have occupied at the beginning of the campaign without opposition. So far as the two armies, with which the campaign was opened, were concerned, he had sustained a defeat, and, if the contest had been between those two armies alone, his would have been destroyed. But, unfortunately, he had the means of reinforcing and recruiting his army to an almost unlimited extent, and there were no means of recruiting General Lee's. Four years of an unexampled struggle had destroyed the finances of the Confederate Government, and exhausted the material out of which an army could be raised. General Lee had performed his task as a military commander, but the Government was unable to furnish him the means of properly continuing the war; and he had therefore to begin the campaign of 1865 with the remnant of his army of the previous year, while a new draft, and heavy reinforcements from other quarters, had furnished his opponent with a new army and largely increased numbers. The few detailed men sent to General Lee, after the revocation of their details, added nothing to the strength of his army, but were a positive injury to it. The mass of them had desired to keep out of the service, because they had no stomach for the fight, and when forced into it, they but served to disseminate dissatisfaction in the ranks of the army. Some writers who never exposed their own precious persons to the bullets of the enemy, have written very glibly about the desertions from the army. Now God forbid that I should say one word in justification of desertion under any circumstances. I had no toleration for it during the war, and never failed to sanction and order the execution of sentences for the extreme penalty for that offence, when submitted to me; but some palliation was to be found for the conduct of many of those who did desert, in the fact that they did

so to go to the aid of their families, who they knew were suffering for the necessaries of life, while many able bodied young men remained at home, in peace and plenty, under exemptions and details. The duty to defend one's country exists independently of any law, and the latter is made to enforce, not create, the obligation. By the law, or the unwise administration of it, a man may be exempted from enforced service, but he cannot be released from the sacred duty of defending his country against invasion. Those able bodied men who flocked abroad to avoid service, and were so blatant in their patriotism when beyond the reach of danger, as I have had occassion to learn in my wanderings, as well as those who sought exemptions and details under the law, with a view to avoid the dangers and hardships of the war, were to all intents and purposes deserters, and morally more criminal than the poor soldier, who, in the agony of his distress for the sufferings of his wife and little ones at home, yielded to the temptation to abandon his colours. There were some cases of exemptions and details, where the persons obtaining them could be more useful at home than in the field, and those who sought them honestly on that account are not subject to the above strictures, but there were many cases where the motives were very different. The men whose names form the roll of honour for the armies of the Confederate States, are those who voluntarily entered the service in the beginning of the war, or as soon as they were able to bear arms, and served faithfully to the end, or until killed or disabled ; and I would advise the unmarried among my fair countrywomen to choose their husbands from among the survivors of this class, and not from among the skulkers. By following this advice, they may not obtain as much pelf, but they may rest assured that they will not be the mothers of cowards, and their posterity will have no cause to blush for the conduct of their progenitors.

OPERATIONS IN 1865.

On the 2nd of January 1865, I had a consultation with Gen. Lee at Richmond, about the difficulties of my position in the Valley, and he told me that he had left me there with the small command which still remained, in order to produce the impression that the force was much larger than it really was, and he instructed me to do the best I could.

Before I returned from Richmond, Rosser started, with between 300 and 400 picked cavalry, for the post of Beverly in Western Virginia, and, on the 11th, surprised and captured the place, securing over five hundred prisoners and some stores. This expedition was made over a very mountainous country, amid the snows of an unusually severe winter. Rosser's loss was very light, but Lieutenant Colonel Cook of the 8th Virginia cavalry, a most gallant and efficient officer, lost his leg in the attack, and had to be left behind.

The great drought during the summer of 1864, had made the corn crop in the Valley a very short one, and, as Sheridan had destroyed a considerable quantity of small grain and hay, I found it impossible to sustain the horses of my cavalry and artillery where they were, and forage could not be obtained from elsewhere. I was therefore compelled to send Fitz Lee's two brigades to General Lee, and Lomax's cavalry was brought from across the Blue Ridge, where the country was exhausted of forage, and sent west into the counties of Pendleton, Highland, Bath, Alleghany, and Greenbrier, where hay could be obtained. Rosser's brigade had to be temporarily disbanded, and the men allowed to go to their homes with their horses, to sustain them, with orders to report when called on.—One or two companies, whose homes were down the

Valley, being required to picket and scout in front of New Market. The men and horses of Lieutenant Colonel King's artillery were sent to South Western Virginia to be wintered, and most of the horses of the other battalions were sent off, under care of some of the men, who undertook to forage them until spring. Nelson's battalion, with some pieces of artillery with their horses, was retained with me, and the remaining officers and men of the other battalions were sent, under the charge of Colonel Carter, to General Lee, to man stationary batteries on his lines. Brigadier General Long, who had been absent on sick leave for some time and had returned, remained with me, and most of the guns which were without horses were sent to Lynchburg by railroad. This was a deplorable state of things, but it could not be avoided, as the horses of the cavalry and artillery would have perished had they been kept in the Valley.

Echols' brigade of Wharton's division was subsequently sent to South Western Virginia, to report to General Echols for special duty, and McNeil's company of partizan rangers and Woodson's company of unattached Missouri cavalry were sent to the County of Hardy—Major Harry Gilmor being likewise ordered to that County, with the remnant of his battalion, to take charge of the whole, and operate against the Baltimore and Ohio railroad ; but he was surprised and captured there, at a private house, soon after his arrival. Two very small brigades of Wharton's division, and Nelson's battalion with the few pieces of artillery which had been retained, were left as my whole available force, and these were in winter quarters near Fishersville, on the Central railroad between Staunton and Waynesboro. The telegraph to New Market and the signal stations from there to the lower Valley were kept up, and a few scouts sent to the rear of the enemy, and in this way was my front principally picketed, and I kept advised of the enemy's movements. Henceforth my efficient and energetic signal officer, Captain Wilburn, was the commander of my advance picket line.

The winter was a severe one, and all material operations

were suspended until its close. Late in February, Lieutenant Jesse McNeil, who was in command of his father's old company, with forty or fifty men of that company and Woodson's, made a dash into Cumberland, Maryland, at night, and captured and brought off Major Generals Crook and Kelly with a staff officer of the latter, though there were at the time several thousand troops in and around Cumberland. The father of this gallant young officer had performed many daring exploits during the war, and had accompanied me into Maryland, doing good service. When Sheridan was at Harrisonburg in October 1864, Captain McNeil had burned the bridge at Edinburg in his rear, and had attacked and captured the guard at the bridge at Mount Jackson, but in this affair he received a very severe wound from which he subsequently died. Lieutenant Baylor of Rosser's brigade, who was in Jefferson County with his company, made one or two dashes on the enemy's outposts during the winter, and, on one occasion, captured a train loaded with supplies, on the Baltimore and Ohio railroad.

On the 20th of February, an order was issued by Gen. Lee, extending my command over the Department of South Western Virginia and East Tennessee, previously commanded by General Breckenridge—the latter having been made Secretary of War.

On the 27th, Sheridan started from Winchester up the Valley with a heavy force, consisting according to the statement of Grant, in his report, of "two divisions of cavalry, numbering about 5,000 each." I had been informed of the preparations for a movement of some kind, some days previous, and the information had been telegraphed to General Lee. As soon as Sheridan started, I was informed of the fact by signal and telegraph, and orders were immediately sent by telegraph to Lomax, whose headquarters were at Millboro, on the Central railroad, forty miles west of Staunton, to get together all of his cavalry as soon as possible. Rosser was also directed to collect all of his men that he could, and an order was sent by telegraph to General Echols, in South-western Virginia, to send his brigade by rail to Lynchburg. My own headquarters were at Staunton, but there were no troops at that place except a local provost guard, and a company of reserves, composed of boys under 18 years of age, which was acting under the orders of the Conscript Bureau. Orders were therefore given for the immediate removal of all stores from that place. Rosser succeeded in collecting a little over 100 men, and with these he attempted to check the enemy at North River, near Mount Grawford, on the 1st of March, but was unable to do so. On the afternoon of that day, the enemy approached to within three or four miles of Staunton, and I then telegraphed to Lomax to concentrate his cavalry at Pound Gap, in Rockbridge County, and to follow and annoy the enemy should he move towards Lynchburg, and rode out of town towards Waynesboro, after all the stores had been removed.

Wharton and Nelson were ordered to move to Waynesboro by light next morning, and on that morning (the 2nd) their commands were put in position on a ridge covering Waynesboro on the west, and just outside of the town. My object, in taking this position, was to secure the removal of five pieces of artillery for which there were no horses, and some stores still in Waynesboro, as well as to present a bold front to the enemy, and ascertain the object of his movement, which I could not do very well if I took refuge at once in the mountain. The last report for Wharton's command showed 1,200 men for duty; but, as it was exceedingly inclement, and raining and freezing, there were not more than 1,000 muskets on the line, and Nelson had six pieces of artillery. I did not intend making my final stand on this ground, yet I was satisfied that if my men would fight, which I had no reason to doubt, I could hold the enemy in check until night, and then cross the river and take position in Rockfish Gap; for I had done more difficult things than that during the war. About 12 o'clock in the day, it was reported to me that the enemy was advancing, and I rode out at once on the lines, and soon discovered about a brigade of cavalry coming up, on the road from Staunton, on which the artillery opened, when it retired out of range. The enemy manœuvred for some time in our front, keeping out of reach of our guns until late in the afternoon, when I discovered a force moving to our left. I immediately sent a messenger with notice of this fact to General Wharton, who was on that flank, and with orders for him to look out and provide for the enemy's advance ; and another messenger, with notice to the guns on the left, and directions for them to fire towards the advancing force, which could not be seen from where they were. The enemy soon made an attack on our left flank, and I discovered the men on that flank giving back. Just then, General Wharton, who had not received my message, rode up to me and I pointed out to him the disorder in his line, and ordered him to ride immediately to that point and rectify it. Before he got back, the troops gave way on the left, after making very slight resistance, and soon everything was in a state of confusion and the men commenced crossing the river. I rode across it myself to try and stop them at the bridge and check the enemy, but they could not be rallied, and the enemy forded the river above and got in our rear. I now saw that everything was lost, and, after the enemy had got between the mountain and the position where I was, and retreat was thus cut off, I rode aside into the woods, and in that way escaped capture. I went to the top of a hill to reconnoitre, and had the mortification of seeing the greater part of my command being carried off as prisoners, and a force of the enemy moving rapidly towards Rockfish Gap. I then rode with the greater part of my staff and 15 or 20 others, including General Long, across the mountain, north of the Gap, with the hope of arriving at Greenwood depot, to which the stores had been removed, before the enemy reached that place ; but, on getting near it, about dark, we discovered the enemy in possession. We then rode to Jarman's Gap, about three miles from the depot, and remained there all night, as the night was exceedingly dark, and the ice rendered it impossible for us to travel over the rugged roads.

The only solution of this affair which I can give, is that my men did not fight as I had expected them to do. Had they done so, I am satisfied that the enemy could have been repulsed ; and I was and still am of opinion that the attack at Waynesboro was a mere demonstration, to cover a movement to the south towards Lynchburg. Yet some excuse is to be made for my men, as they knew that they were weak and the enemy very strong.

The greater part of my command was captured, as was also the artillery, which, with five guns on the cars at Greenwood, made eleven pieces. Very few were killed or wounded on either side. The only person killed on our side, that I have ever heard of, was Colonel William H. Harman, who had formerly been in the army, but then held a civil appointment ; and he was shot in the streets of Waynesboro, either after he had been made prisoner, as some said, or while he was attempting to make his escape after everything was over. My aide, Lieut. Wm. G. Calloway, who had been sent to the left with one of the messages, and my medical director, Surgeon H. McGuire, had the misfortune to fall into the hands of the enemy. All the waggons of Wharton's command were absent getting supplies; but those we had with us, including the ordnance and medical waggons, and my own baggage waggon, fell into the hands of the enemy.*

On the 3rd, I rode, with the party that was with me, to-

---

* Grant, in speaking of this affair, says : "He (Sheridan) entered Staunton on the 2nd, the enemy having retreated on Waynesboro. Thence he pushed on to Waynesboro, where he found the enemy in force in an entrenched position, under General Early. Without stopping to make a reconnoissance, an immediate attack was made, the position was carried, and 1,600 prisoners, 11 pieces of artillery, with horses and caissons complete, 200 waggons and teams loaded with subsistence, and 17 battle-flags, were captured." This is all very brilliant; but, unfortunately for its truth, Sheridan was not at Waynesboro, but was at Staunton, where he had stopped with a part of his force ; while the affair at Waynesboro was conducted by one of his subordinates. The strength of my force has already been stated, and it was not in an entrenched position. I am not able to say how many prisoners were taken, but I know that they were more than my command numbered, as a very considerable number of recently exchanged and paroled prisoners were at the time in the Valley, on leave of absence from General Lee's army. I not only did not have 200 waggons or anything like it, but had no use for them. Where the 17 battle-flags could have been gotten, I cannot imagine.

wards Charlottesville ; but, on getting near that place, we found the enemy entering it. We had then to turn back and go by a circuitous route under the mountains to Gordonsville, as the Rivanna River and other streams were very much swollen. On arriving at Gordonsville, I found General Wharton, who had made his escape to Charlottesville on the night of the affair at Waynesboro, and he was ordered to Lynchburg, by the way of the Central and South-Side railroads, to take command of Echols' brigade, and aid in the defence of the city. General Long was ordered to report to General Lee at Petersburg.

The affair at Waynesboro diverted Sheridan from Lynchburg, which he could have captured without difficulty, had he followed Hunter's route and not jumped at the bait unwillingly offered him, by the capture of my force at the former place. His deflection from the direct route to the one by Charlottesville, was without adequate object, and resulted in the abandonment of the effort to capture Lynchburg, or to cross the James River to the south side. He halted at Charlottesville for two or three days, and then moved towards James River below Lynchburg, when, being unable to cross that river, he crossed over the Rivanna, at its mouth, and then moved by the way of Frederick's Hall on the Central railroad, and Ashland on the R. F. & P. railroad, across the South and North Annas, and down the Pamunkey to the White House.

At Gordonsville, about 200 cavalry were collected under Col. Morgan of the 1st. Virginia Cavalry, and, with this force, I watched the enemy for several days while he was at Charlottesville, and when he was endeavouring to cross the James River. When Sheridan had abandoned this effort, and on the day he reached the vicinity of Ashland, while I was riding on the Louisa Court House and Richmond road, towards the bridge over the South Anna, with about 20 cavalry, I came very near being captured, by a body of 300 cavalry sent after me, but I succeeded in eluding the enemy with most of those who were with me, and reached Richmond at two o'clock next morning, after passing twice between the enemy's camps and his pickets. My Adjutant General, Captain Moore, how ever, was captured, but made his escape.

Lomax had succeeded in collecting a portion of his cavalry and reaching Lynchburg, where he took position on the north bank of the river, but the enemy avoided that place. Rosser had collected a part of his brigade and made an attack, near New Market, on the guard which was carrying back the prisoners captured at Waynesboro, with the view of releasing them, but he did not succeed in that object, though the guard was compelled to retire in great haste. He then moved towards Richmond on Sheridan's track.

After consultation with General Lee, at his head-quarters near Petersburg, Rosser's and McCausland's brigades were ordered to report to him under the command of General Rosser, and I started for the Valley, by the way of Lynchburg, to reorganize what was left of my command. At Lynchburg, a despatch was received from General Echols, stating that Thomas was moving in East Tennessee, and threatening South Western Virginia with a heavy force, and I immediately went on the cars to Wytheville. From that place I went with General Echols to Bristol, on the state line between Virginia and Tennessee, and it was ascertained beyond doubt that some important movement by the enemy was on foot. We then returned to Abingdon, and while I was engaged in endeavouring to organize the small force in that section, so as to meet the enemy in the best way we could, I received, on the 30th March, a telegraphic despatch from General Lee, directing me to turn over the command in South Western Virginia to General Echols, and in the Valley to General Lomax, and informing me that he would address a letter to me at my home. I complied at once with this order, and thus terminated my military career.

CONCLUSION.

In the afternoon of the 30th March, after having turned over the command to General Echols, I rode to Marion in Smythe County, and was taken that night with a cold and cough so violent as to produce hemorrhage from the lungs, and prostrate me for several days in a very dangerous condition. While I was in this situation, a heavy cavalry force under Stoneman, from Thomas' army in Tennessee, moved through North Carolina to the east, and a part of it came into Virginia from the main column, and struck the Virginia and Tennessee rail-road at New River, east of Wytheville; whence, after destroying the bridge, it moved east, cutting off all communication with Richmond, and then crossed over into North Carolina. As soon as I was in a condition to be moved, I was carried on the railroad to Wytheville, and was proceeding thence to my home, in an ambulance under the charge of a surgeon, when I re ceived, most unexpectedly, the news of the surrender of General Lee's army. Without the slightest feeling of irreverence, I will say, that the sound of the last trump would not have been more unwelcome to my ears.

Under the disheartening influence of the sad news I had received, I proceeded to my home, and I subsequently received a letter from General Lee, dated on the 30th of March, explaining the reasons for relieving me from command. As a copy of that letter has been published in Virginia, without any knowledge or agency on my part, it is appended to this narrative. The letter itself, which was written on the very day of the commencement of the attack on General Lee's lines which resulted in the evacuation of Richmond, and just ten days before the surrender of the Army of Northern Virginia, has a historical interest; for it shows that our great commander, even at that late day, was anxiously and earnestly contemplating the continuation of the struggle with unabated vigour, and a full determination to make available every element of success.

Immediately after the battle of Cedar Creek, I had written a letter to General Lee, stating my willingness to be relieved from command, if he deemed it necessary for the public interests, and I should have been content with the course pursued towards me, had his letter not contained the expressions of personal confidence in me which it does; for I knew that, in everything he did as commander of our armies, General Lee was actuated solely by an earnest and ardent desire for the success of the cause of his country. As to those among my countrymen who judged me harshly, I have not a word of reproach. When there was so much at stake, it was not unnatural that persons entirely ignorant of the facts, and forming their opinions from the many false reports set afloat in a time of terrible war and public suffering, should pass erroneous and severe judgments on those commanders who met with reverses.

I was not embraced in the terms of General Lee's surrender or that of General Johnston, and, as the order relieving me from command had also relieved me from all embarrassment as to the troops which had been under me, as soon as I was in a condition to travel, I started on horse-back for the Trans-Mississipi Department, to join the army of General Kirby Smith, should it hold out; with the hope of at least meeting an honorable death while fighting under the flag of my country. Before I reached that Department, Smith's army had also been surrendered, and, without giving a parole or incurring any obligation whatever to the United States authorities, after a long, weary, and dangerous ride from Virginia, through the States of North Carolina, South Carolina, Georgia, Alabama, Mississippi, Arkansas and Texas, I finally succeeded in leaving the country; a voluntary exile rather than submit to the rule of our enemies.

J. A. EARLY

APPENDIX.

A.

LETTER FROM GENERAL LEE.

"Hd. Qrs., C. S. Armies,
"30th March, 1865.

"Lt.-General J. A. Early, Franklin Co., Va.

"General,—My telegram will have informed you that I deem a change of Commanders in your Department necessary; but it is due to your zealous and patriotic services that I should explain the reasons that prompted my action. The situation of affairs is such that we can neglect no means calculated to devolop the resources we possess to the greatest extent, and make them as efficient as possible. To this end, it is essential that we should have the cheerful and hearty support of the people, and the full confidence of the soldiers, without which our efforts would be embarrassed and our means of resistance weakened. I have reluctantly arrived at the conclusion that you cannot command the united and willing co-operation which is so essential to success. Your reverses in the Valley, of which the public and the army judge chiefly by the results, have, I fear, impaired your influence both with the people and the soldiers, and would add greatly to the difficulties which will, under any circumstances, attend our military operations in S. W. Virginia. While my own confidence in your ability, zeal, and devotion to the cause is unimpaired, I have nevertheless felt that I could not oppose what seems to be the current of opinion, without injustice to your reputation and injury to the service. I therefore felt constrained to endeavour to find a commander who would be more likely to develop the strength and resources of the country, and inspire tbe soldiers with confidence; and, to accomplish this purpose, I thought it proper to yield my own opinion, and to defer to that of those to whom alone we can look for support.

I am sure that you will understand and appreciate my motives, and no one will be more ready than yourself to acquiesce in any measures which the interests of the country may seem to require, regardless of all personal considerations.

Thanking you for the fidelity and energy with which you have always supported my efforts, and for the courage and devotion you have ever manifested in the service of the country,

I am, very respectfully and truly,

Your ob't serv't,

R. E. LEE,

Gen'l."

———

Since the foregoing narrative was written, I have seen, in a newspaper published in the United States, the following communication:—

"HD. QRS., BATTALION U. S. INFANTRY,

" Camp near Lynchburg, Va.,

" Feb. 7, 1866.

" C. W. BUTTON, Esq., Editor Lynchburg Virginian.

" SIR,—I have received a communication from the War Department, Adjutant-General's Office, relative to a newspaper slip, containing a copy of General Lee's letter to General Early, on removing him from command. The letter is dated Headquarters C. S. Armies, March 30, addressed to Lieut.-Gen. Early, Franklin C. H., Virginia, and is said to be in your possession, it having appeared in your paper. The Secretary of War considers that the original letter properly belongs to the Archive office.

I am directed by Major-General Terry, commanding this Department, to procure said letter, and I therefore call your attention to the matter, and request that you deliver to me the original letter in your possession, in compliance with my instructions.

I am, very respectfully, your obedient servant,

A. E. LATIMER,

Brevet Major and Captain 11th U. S. Infantry,

Commanding Post."

This demand for General Lee's private letter to me, and the attempt to enforce it by military power, show how wide has been the departure from the original principles of the United States Government, and to what petty and contemptible measures that Government, as at present administered, resorts in domineering over a disarmed and helpless people. I have the pleasure of informing the Hon. Secretary of War, and the keeper of the "Archive Office," that the original letter is in my possession, beyond the reach of provost marshals and agents of the Freedman's Bureau, or even Holt with his Bureau of Military Justice and his suborners of perjury.

B.

STATISTICS SHOWING THE RELATIVE STRENGTH OF THE TWO SECTIONS DURING THE WAR.

The census of the United States for 1860 showed an aggregate free population of 27,185,109 ; of this, 488,283 were free blacks, of which the larger proportion were in the Southern States, but it is not necessary to consider that element in this estimate, though to do so would make it more favourable for the Confederate States. Of the above 27,185,109 of free population, there were in the States forming the Southern Confederacy, as follows :—

Alabama	529,164
Arkansas	324,323
Florida	78,686
Georgia	595,097
Kentucky	930,223
Louisiana	376,913
Mississippi	354,699
Missouri	1,058,352
North Carolina	661,586
South Carolina	301,271
Tennessee	834,063
Texas	420,651
Virginia	1,105,196
Aggregate	7,570,224

Kentucky undertook to assume a neutral position, but she was soon overrun by Federal troops, and her government and a very large proportion of her population took sides with the North. Those of her citizens who were not awed by Federal bayonets, formed a state government and joined the Confederacy—many of her young men going into the Confederate army ; but in fact, whatever may have been the sympathies of the people, her moral influence as well as the benefit of her physical strength were given to the Federal Government. The legitimate Government of Missouri sided with the South, as very probably did the majority of her people, but she was also overrun at a very early stage of the war by Federal troops, and her legitimate Government subverted by force; and the benefit of her resources and physical strength was likewise given to the United States, notwithstanding the fact that a large number of her men joined the Confederate army. Perhaps the number of men added to the strength of the Confederate army from Kentucky and Missouri, did not acceed the accession to the Federal army from Western Virginia, Eastern Tennessee, and some other of the Southern States, and that, in estimating the relative strength of the two parties at the beginning, it would be proper to reject Kentucky and Missouri from the estimate of the Confederate strength. The free population of these two States amounted to 1,988,575, and without them there would be left on the Confederate side a free population of 5,581,649 against a similar population of 21,603,460 on the Federal side, which would make the odds against us very nearly four to one :—but I will divide the population of these States equally between the parties, and this will give a free population of 6,575,937 Confederates, against a similar population of 20,609,172 Federals, which makes the odds more than three to one against us in the beginning, without considering the fact that the Northern people had possession of the Government, with the army and navy and all the resources of that Government, while the Confederate States had to organize a new Government, and provide an army and the means of supplying it with arms as well as every thing else. Notwithstanding this immense odds against us, I presume there is scarcely a Confederate, even now, who does not feel confident that if it had been, " hands off and a fair fight," we would have prevailed ; but an immense horde of foreign mercenaries, incited by high bounties and the hope of plunder held out to them, flocked to the Federal army ; and thus was its size continually growing, while the Confederate army had to rely on the original population to keep up its strength. Any accession of troops from Maryland was more than counterbalanced by those obtained from Western Virginia by the Federals, without counting East Tennessee or other quarters. The Federal Government was not satisfied with recruiting its army from abroad, but, as the country was overrun, the southern negroes were forced into its service, and thus, by the aid of its foreign mercenaries and the negro recruits, it was enabled finally to exhaust the Confederate army.

To show the immense strength of the Federal army, the following extracts are taken from the report of the Federal Secretary of War, Stanton, which was sent to the Congress at its session beginning on the first Monday in December, 1865. In that report he says : —

" Official reports show that on the 1st of May, 1864, the aggregate national military force of all arms, officers and men, was nine hundred and seventy thousand seven hundred and ten, to wit :—

Available force present for duty	662,345
On detached service in the different military departments.	109,348
In field hospitals or unfit for duty	41,266
In general hospitals or on sick leave at home	75,978
Absent on furlough or as prisoners of war	66,290
Absent without leave	15,483
Grand aggregate	970,710

"The aggregate available force present for duty May 1st, 1864, was distributed in the different commands as follows :—

Department of Washington	42 124
Army of the Potomac	120,386
Department of Virginia and North Carolina	59,139
Department of the South	18,165
Department of the Gulf	61,865
Department of Arkansas	23,666
Department of the Tennessee	74,174
Department of the Missouri	15,770
Department of the North-West	5,295
Department of Kansas	4,798
Head-quarters Military Division of the Mississippi	476
Department of the Cumberland	119,948
Department of the Ohio	35,416
Northern Department	9,540
Department of West Virginia	30,782
Department of the East	2,828
Department of the Susquehanna	2,970
Middle Department	5,627
Ninth Army Corps	20,780
Department of New Mexico	3,454
Deprrtment of the Pacific	5,141
Total	662,345."

And again :—

" Official reports show that on the 1st of March, 1865, the aggregate military force of all arms, officers and men, was nine hundred and sixty-five thousand five hundred and ninety-one, to wit :—

Available force present for duty	602,598
On detached service in the different military departments.	132,538
In field hospitals and unfit for duty....................	35,628
In general hospitals or on sick leave..................	143,419
Absent on furlough or as prisoners of war........... .	31,695
Absent without leave...............................	19,683
Grand aggregate	965.591

"This force was augmented on the 1st of May, 1865, by enlistments, to the number of one million five hundred and sixteen of all arms, officers and men, (1,000,516)."

And again he says :—

"The aggregate quotas charged against the several States, under all calls made by the President of the United States, from the 15th day of April, 1861, to the 14th day of April, 1865, at which time drafting and recruiting ceased, was.. 2,759,049
"The aggregate number of men credited on the several calls, and put into service of the United States, in the army, navy, and marine corps, during the above period, was 2,656,553
"Leaving a deficiency on all calls, when the war closed, of 102,596 "

This does not include that portion of the Federal forces consisting of the regular army, and the negro troops raised in the Southern States ; which were not raised by calls on the States. It is impossible for me to state the number of troops called into the service of the Confederate Government during the war, as all its records fell into the hands of the United States authorities, or were destroyed, but I think I can safely assert that the "available force present for duty" in the Federal army, at the beginning* or close of the last year of the war, exceeded the entire force called into the Confederate service during the whole war ; and when it is considered that the troops called into the United States service during that time, numbered more than one-third of the entire free population of the Confederate States, men, women and children, the world can appreciate the profound ability of the leaders, and the great heroism of the soldiers, of that army which finally overcame the Confederate army, by the "mere attrition" of numbers, after a prolonged struggle of four years. They can be excelled only by the *magnanimity* of the conquerors.